Lost and Found

A volume in the CounterCulture Series
Also available:
   Rebel Music: The Harvey Kubernik InnerViews by Harvey Kubernik
   New Buffalo: Journals from a Taos Commune by Arthur Kopecky

Editors: David Farber, History, University of New Mexico
         Beth L. Bailey, American Studies, University of New Mexico

Lost and Found

my life in a
group marriage
commune

Margaret Hollenbach

University of New Mexico Press
Albuquerque

09   08   07   06   05   04   1   2   3   4   5

Library of Congress Cataloging-in-Publication Data

Hollenbach, Margaret, 1944–

Lost and found : my life in a group marriage commune /
Margaret Hollenbach.—1st ed.

p. cm. — (CounterCulture series)

ISBN 0-8263-3463-6 (pbk : alk. paper)

   1. Hollenbach, Margaret, 1944–

   2. Hippies—United States—Biography.

   3. Young women—United States—Biography.

   4. The Family (Taos, N.M. : Commune)

   5. Communal living—New Mexico—Taos.

   6. Group marriage—New Mexico—Taos.

   7. Counterculture—New Mexico—Taos.

   I. Title. II. Series.

HQ971.5.N7H65 2004

307.77'4'092—dc22

2004005358

Wilhelm, Richard: *The I Ching, Or Book of Changes* (Third
Edition). © 1967 Princeton University Press, 1995 Renewed
PUP. Reprinted by permission of Princeton University Press.

Printed and bound in the USA by Edwards Brothers, Inc.

Typeset in Garamond MT 11/14

Display type set in Frutiger Condensed and Dave's Hand

Design and composition: Robyn Mundy

Contents

Preface

In 1970, I joined a commune in Taos, New Mexico. I had dropped out of graduate school in cultural anthropology at the University of Washington the year before, and had suffered some losses that propelled me out of Seattle on a search for adventure. I met two representatives of a commune called The Family at the World Affairs Conference in Boulder, Colorado and decided to change my name, give up my possessions, and join them.[1]

After leaving the Family, considerably changed, I sought out a man whose books I had admired in college and graduate school. He and his wife took me into their extended family circle and encouraged me to write about my experience. I turned the story into a master's thesis and a means of rejoining graduate school. The master's thesis was an analysis of the social organization of the commune, titled "Commune or Cult? The Family of Taos, New Mexico." An excerpt was published in *Communes: Creating and Managing the Collective Life*, edited by Rosabeth Kanter, a sociologist at Brandeis University.

Thus, graduate school in cultural anthropology bracketed my adventures in dropping out; but I think it was in the Family that I learned that anthropology is not, and no science can be, a complete worldview. While I am satisfied that I wrote an accurate description of how the Family worked at the time I was a member, I tabled a discussion of why I joined,

---

1. More than one communal group has taken that name. The Taos Family is not related to others that I know of.

what really happened to me on an emotional level, why I left, and what I learned. My experience in the Taos Family remained an undigested lump somewhere in the back of my mind.

For years I was ashamed of myself for having chosen, when so many communes formed, a group that turned out to have millenarian beliefs that I thought were foolish and a charismatic leader who, in spite of all that was said about his reluctance to lead and his voluntary giving up of power, wielded considerable authority and gave the group the characteristics of a cult.

What is a cult? I don't think it's important to define the word. I think the more important questions are, "How closed is this group?" and "How easy is it to leave?"

Theoretically, it was easy to join and easy to leave the Family. It was said that "Anyone who is willing to live as we do can join," and "We never ask anyone to leave." The correlate was that anyone who didn't like being there could simply walk away. On the other hand, the Family was psychologically rather closed. Any small group can become that way, the more its members interact exclusively, intensely, or round-the-clock with each other. A small, enclosed group can take off in any direction and carry a set of beliefs, feelings, or values to an illogical extreme. We did that, as did many American communes at the time.

For me, it was physically easy but emotionally excruciating to leave. I desperately wanted the companionship and joy of living together with people my own age in that beautiful place. But I wasn't willing to pay the price. That is the third important question about membership in any group: "What's the price?"

The Family's price was higher than I realized at the outset. It was more than the explicit rules: change your name, give up all your possessions, use no drugs, settle all conflicts by face-to-face hassling. In addition, give up all your privacy, including whatever you say to anyone here; do whatever the leader or the group decides for you; and for the women, have sex with the leader whenever he requests it; accept everything he says; live with the consequences of his decisions.

When I set out to write this book, I thought I was only telling a personal story. I had no idea how much it would help me grow, nor did I realize that it would ultimately show me how much my own life was intertwined with the century's. The dates that frame my parents' lives and my own determined so much of what we thought, felt, and did. So many of my agemates were influenced, as I was, by the Beat poets, existentialism, the American interpreters of Zen Buddhism, *Mad* magazine, David Brower, sociology and anthropology, *The Teachings of Don Juan*, Timothy Leary, Ram Dass, the alternative media, and the psychological, political, and spiritual issues that formed the motivation for the counterculture.

It is humbling to discover that one is thoroughly a creature of one's times, especially for people of my generation, raised to believe that we were unique and powerful enough to create something entirely new. It is humbling but also enormously comforting, like finding a community of the soul.

The Family took a large helping of its inspiration from Gestalt therapy, as developed by Fritz Perls, although I don't think Perls would have liked what he saw. The "Gestalt sessions" in the Family often turned toward mindfucking and accusations. Nevertheless, there was a seed of truth there, and a commitment to being fully present, being in the now, that is the essence of the spiritual teachings now flooding our parched culture. I use the word *culture*, still, as anthropologists do, to mean the vast texture of things we take for granted, of shared meanings, understandings, and practices that arise in an interacting human group. Part of our culture is what Viktor Frankl called "the existential vacuum that is the mass neurosis of the present time . . . a private and personal form of nihilism."

It's hard to live as a nihilist. Lord Sean, one of the Family's representatives in Boulder, said that when he met me I was "in the Void." He was right. I was stumbling around in the void of meaning that my family, community, education, and century created for me, and besides that, I thought I was screwed up, a magically self-fulfilling belief. I was looking for "a path with heart," thanks to another graduate student in anthropology, Carlos Castañeda. My path with heart took me into, and out of, the Family.

Humanistic psychology offered many paths to self-discovery, and I explored some of them before joining the Family. I also dropped out of graduate school once before. During that time I worked for the *Los Angeles Free Press*, took LSD, drove cross-country visiting relatives and friends, lived in Santa Fe for a month, considered checking myself into the New Mexico state mental hospital (but didn't), and, finally, returned to graduate school, only to leave again to work for Seattle's first non-commercial radio station, KRAB-FM.

Although much of that experience was fun, from my perspective in my fifty-ninth year, looking back, I would say that I was twisting and turning, desperately seeking something for which I didn't have a name and could therefore only search randomly. But I was not alone in that search, nor is it so unusual among young people now. What the Family showed me, and showed me well, were some of the paths I couldn't take to resolve my own questions of meaning. Most of all, I couldn't choose a path with heart that excluded a path with critical thinking. I agree with journalist Nicholas Kristof who wrote that "the heart is a wonderful organ, but so is the brain." Both must come along on any life journey.

And a proviso: This story is half-true. It's my true half, as I remember it, of the relationships and events I took part in while I was a member of the Family commune of Taos, New Mexico in spring 1970. I have filled in details and even created scenes to convey what I felt and remembered. I have changed most of the names, even though the names used while I was there were not the members' legal names and are probably not their names now. I do not know where they are today.[2]

2. Journalists interviewed members of the Family more than once during the peak of interest in New Mexico communes. Two books contain chapters on the Family: *Communes USA: A Personal Tour*, by Richard Fairfield, Penguin Books, Inc., Baltimore, Maryland, 1972, and *Armed Love*, by Elia Katz, Bantam Books, Holt, Rinehart and Winston, New York, 1971.

Let that feeling be there

1

Now let me tell you of a dilemma which is not easy to understand. It's like a koan—those Zen questions which seem to be insoluble. The koan is: **Nothing exists except the here and now.** . . . *Some people then make a program out of this. They make a demand, 'You should live in the here and now.' And I say it's not possible to live in the here and now, and yet, nothing exists except the here and now.*

—Frederick S. Perls, *Gestalt Therapy Verbatim*
(1992, The Center for Gestalt Development), p. 61

Group marriage, with its suggestion of abundant sex, wasn't what attracted me to the commune; it was the idea of living among fifty people my own age and the hope that some of them might love me. When Lord Sean peered down at me, all elbows and grin, and asked, "Are you ready?" I nodded like a swimmer accepting the current. He folded me into his arms and hugged me tight. His yellow beanie fell to the floor.

I looked into his eyes, gleaming and magnified by his glasses. The beanie had mashed his hair down on top, and now it stuck out on both sides. With his wide, smiling mouth and lanky body, he looked like an upright grasshopper.

"I've been alone all my life," I said, catching my breath. "The thought of having fifty brothers and sisters makes me feel like a kid in a candy store."

"Ah, you have a good heart," he said.

I couldn't remember my heart being mentioned outside of a doctor's office. In my family we used phrases such as "have a heart" or "you're breaking my heart," but we didn't talk much about the simple moments of the heart that seemed easy for Lord Sean and his companion, Lady Samantha. The fact that he thought I had a good heart pulled me even further in.

"Somebody who wants to join that bad should be able to," he said. "You can leave with us for Taos in the morning." Lady Samantha hugged me, too, enveloping me in the smell of patchouli. That night I packed up some clothes, a sleeping bag, and my camera, and said goodbye to my fellow workers at Fred's Steak House in Boulder. It was April 1970. I was twenty-five.

The year before that, several key things in my life had fallen apart within a few months: I lost the best job I'd ever had, broke up with my lover, Jeffrey, barely escaped death at the hands of a serial killer, and then my therapist, a kind old man from Vienna, died a week after advising me to leave town.

At the time, I lived in a one-room apartment that opened onto an alley on Seattle's Capital Hill. The man who lived upstairs was a graphic artist. A poster on his door showed a man with the top of his head going up in orange flames. "Aspen International Design Conference," it said, June 15-17, 1969. Buckminster Fuller would attend. Everything about it sounded exciting.

I packed everything I owned into my old, round-backed Volvo and headed for Aspen. In those days, Aspen was a small mountain town, not the rich people's preserve it is now. The air had a special clarity that is probably gone now. It felt like the first day of new glasses, when you've been nearsighted all your life; every leaf, every pine needle, every cloud in the sky leapt into sharp focus and every breath felt perfectly new, never breathed before. The town was small enough to walk or bike anywhere without ever losing sight of the sky or the surrounding granite peaks. When the conference was over, I couldn't bear to leave. I found a job at the Center of the Eye, a fine-arts photography school. The director let me live in a tree house on her property for the summer. When cold weather set in, I moved to Boulder and went to work as a waitress at Fred's Steak House. In those days my life was intense; it would take most of an hour to tell a therapist what happened in my week.

I met Lord Sean and Lady Samantha at the World Affairs Conference in Boulder the next spring. They were invited representatives of a Taos, New Mexico commune called The Family. This conference came along at a point when I was getting restive in my work and my situation. I had dropped out of graduate school in anthropology the year before but hadn't developed any clear notion of what to do instead. My father wrote weekly letters urging me to come home and get a job.

Honey, now that you have given up on the academic bit, I hope you will get better organized and aim for a spot to which you can do justice, and vice versa. I think that the State of California and the southern end particularly offers more opportunity than most any other section of the country. If you want a temporary roost, come down to the house. You have a key and if you can't find it, Lait next door will let you in and there is an extra set of keys for the Comet that has a house key on it.

In looking for a job, you should investigate the civil service lists at all levels. These spots are much better than they were and don't be too choosy at first. Almost any slot is better than none, as you can often progress more easily from a grubby (relatively speaking) inside position than by assaulting from the outside at loftier levels. Money and fringewise, the teaching profession is very good, but there has been a drastic decline in openings lately. That area is a dud at present.

Write, honey. much love, Dad.

Naturally, I ignored his advice. A beginning slot in the civil service wasn't even at the bottom of my list. Nor had I completely given up on academia.

I missed some things about it, especially the conferences. To me, academic conferences were like merry-go-rounds—full of colorful animals, centrifugal motion, and a chance to spin off onto the next ride. My favorite part of graduate school had been the American Anthropological Association's annual meetings. I spent the four or five days of "the Meetings" on a continuous adrenaline high, rushing from one academic paper to the next, and then to an interesting conversation in the hall, or sharing the elevator with Margaret Mead or Tony Wallace or some other high-status professor whose book I had just read. The excitement continued on into the night, from dinner with friends and scholars from all over the world to the parties that followed and the flirtations that sometimes culminated in getting laid, high in a hotel room overlooking some city, an open briefcase on the dresser, cries and murmurs in tune with the whoosh of the building's HVAC system. The Meetings were so exciting that I felt I could spin out into another world, another skin, a dimension of color and texture and pure idea—an intellectual-sensual high.

The World Affairs Conference was a hybrid animal, more akin to the Movement of the sixties than a conventional academic affair. The Movement was more than the struggle for civil rights and opposition to the Vietnam War. It included passionate critiques of capitalism, materialism, and the "military industrial complex," of which Eisenhower, himself a product of it, warned. The Movement contained a fundamental optimism about society and the human spirit; it fostered Utopian dreams. Communes were much in the news at the time, each one a small-group experiment, a refraction of the colors of '60s idealism. All of these ideas found some play in the World Affairs Conference.

An eccentric sociology professor at the University of Colorado, Howard Higman, started the World Affairs Conference in 1948, and ran it according to principles that he believed would make for a wide-open exchange of ideas. The invited presenters were not paid, and were offered lodging in local homes, not hotels. They were encouraged to stay for the entire conference, not just their own sessions, and to participate in the other sessions as members of the audience. This made the conference more intense and created a feeling of community.

The presenters were asked to speak on big questions outside their own expertise and to engage the audience in the discussion. Topics ranged wide and were provocative. Session titles in 1970 included "Disarmament Foreplay"; "An Apology to the Ecology: Macrobiotic

Politics"; "The Nixonization of the Nation: Watergate or Waterlog"; and "Women in the Morning: Motherhood: Voluntary or Mandatory." Presenters included film critic Roger Ebert, journalist Russell Baker, and historian Stanley Hoffman.

The Family was described as "a group marriage based on Gestalt therapy and 24-hour encounter," and was featured in several sessions during the week of the conference. A session called "Communes—The Kibbutz of the Seventies" attracted several hundred people on the conference's second day. Perhaps for most of them group marriage was the draw. For me it was Gestalt therapy and communal living.

Marriage was nothing I wanted. My parents divorced when I was ten, and I hadn't yet seen an intimate relationship that I would want to copy. I used to say that marriage was an agreement between two people to make each other miserable. When a boyfriend early in graduate school suggested we might get married, I got away from him as fast as I could. The idea of a commune, though, had some appeal. I believed it might be possible to create a better way of life than I had experienced as an only child in an American nuclear family. My parents moved every six months when I was a kid, so I never had the long-term friendships or extended family that are the building blocks of communities in most of the world. Part of the fascination of anthropology was the hope of finding a model somewhere of a better way to be human.

In my second year of graduate school, someone told me I needed therapy. Specifically, the wife of a man I was flirting with said she thought I had a problem. I had gone through several men in the first year of graduate school, not particularly happily, but hadn't thought of that as a problem. I did believe there was something wrong with me—I just couldn't figure out what. I found a book that summarized several styles of therapy. Research indicated they all had about the same low rate of success; a more important factor than the theory or method was the personal relationship with the therapist and the perception of shared values.

Gestalt therapy interested me because of its emphasis on present experience. Fritz Perls, its founder, was trained in Freudian analysis but came to reject the idea of probing endlessly into the past. He maintained that by becoming more fully aware of oneself in the present moment, one could change faster. He said the important question was not *why* but *how*—How are you doing, feeling, being, what you are right now? That made sense to me. It also meshed perfectly with the spirit of the times.

Lord Sean, tall, bespectacled, and unkempt, bounded to the front of the auditorium and faced the crowd. Lady Samantha, small and delicate, floated behind him in a floor-length burgundy gown. They both looked to be in their mid-twenties. Sean started by saying that he had a master's degree in psychology and Samantha had dropped out of Vassar. Most members of the commune were well-educated, he said. They didn't mind being called hippies but wanted to make it clear that intelligence and a wider view of the world had gone into their decision to drop out of mainstream society.

"The Family started out in 1967 as a group of friends in Berkeley," Lord Sean said. "We took LSD together and got really close. We shared a vision of a better world, and we wanted to be of service. When Ken Kesey said it was time to 'go beyond LSD and live your vision,' we agreed. But life in the city felt like a dead end."

The group pooled what little money they had and gave it to the man now called "Lord Byron," who believed he could use the group's energy to help him win big in Las Vegas. They sat together in a Haight Ashbury living room, holding hands and praying for him the night he won $12,000 and bankrolled their move from the city. They travelled around for a while before settling on Taos as their new home. They arrived late in 1968, as a wave of young people searching for a better life rolled into this small town.

Taos was predominantly conservative, Hispanic, and Catholic. Despite a healthy sprinkling of artists, writers, and wealthy patrons of the arts, despite the ski resort, Taos County was one of the poorest in the entire country. This town of 2,400 was ill-prepared for an onslaught of new residents, mostly young, Anglo, poor, and, in some sense, radical.

Members of the Family, Sean said, saw themselves as something like hippie social workers. In Taos, they staffed a health food store, helped run a free clinic, and set up an information center for newcomers. They had given up drugs.

"Our goals were to make a group marriage," Lord Sean said, "and save the world."

In other times and places a skinny man in a yellow beanie saying he wanted to save the world might sound foolish or mad. But most of that audience seemed to agree that there was a lot wrong with the world and that it was in need of saving.

I was born in an Army hospital in Pasadena, California, August 6, 1944, one year to the day before the bomb named Little Boy fell on Hiroshima. My father was a supply officer at an army base in San Pedro. My mother, grandmother, and I lived in Ontario, in a 1920s farmhouse surrounded by orange groves. My father came home on the weekends. Perhaps he came home early on August 6, 1945, not just for my birthday, but because of the news. My mother would have made a pineapple upside-down cake, and she might have had one candle to light for me to try to blow out. They would have kept the radio on, and who knows what they would have felt—horror? awe? joy or sorrow? a mixture of both?—about the destruction unleashed on Japan. My father hated the army, but he wasn't a pacifist and probably supported Truman's decision.

Soon after the war ended, my father was discharged from the army and decided to go back to school under the G.I. bill. He studied for a master's degree in bacteriology at the University of Michigan, his alma mater, and we lived in student "barracks," then in an apartment over a store in Okemos, Michigan, then in Wellington, Ohio. I'm not sure why we moved so much. Perhaps he was doing research, or maybe that was when he left graduate school without finishing his thesis in order to take a job. We moved for one reason or another. My mother's seven brothers and sisters and their families all stayed in Michigan, mostly in Detroit, but my father's sisters and mother had settled in Los Angeles. I suppose that set up the tracks we rolled on. He loved California for its climate and its job opportunities. She missed her family. Until they divorced, when I was ten, we moved back and forth between Southern California and Michigan so often that I changed schools twice a year. I was always the new kid.

During the Cold War, whether the school was in Michigan or California, the civil defense drills taught us second and third graders to hide under our desks with our arms over our heads for protection against the blinding flash of the Russian A-bomb. My father scoffed at the drills. Even at that age I understood that no protection could be enough.

I never seriously believed I would live to adulthood. For some reason my mind fastened on the age of seventeen. The end of the world would come right around that time. I was surprised as I reached eighteen, nineteen, twenty, and the years continued ticking off without a terminal explosion. So Lord Sean sounded perfectly right-on to me.

Lady Samantha stepped forward. She had a cloud of curly dark hair that accentuated her small face and air of fragility, but she spoke with confidence. The Family ran on very few rules, she explained: No drugs. Give up all your possessions. Change your name. "Group marriage" meant that each man and woman was committed to all the other members, and all adults were equally responsible for the children.

"We're creating a new kind of society," Samantha said. "It's time for mankind to evolve, and we believe we are part of the new stage."

It crossed my mind to wonder how a group marriage would work. I knew from my courses in anthropology that in most of the rest of the world, people live in households full of relatives, unlike the nuclear family considered normal in the United States. There are usually several adults and/or older children to watch over the younger ones. But these are relatives who have grown up around each other. Would unrelated people who might or might not have experience with young children become good caretakers?

I wondered if group marriage was really new. I knew that marriage, as a long-term sexual and parenting relationship, is a human universal, but I couldn't think of a case exactly like what the Family described. In the Israeli kibbutz, which Samantha said was the closest comparison, child rearing is shared but sex partners are monogamous. In some societies marriage is polygamous (multiple wives) or polyandrous (multiple husbands), but I didn't know of any that were both. Traditionally, among the Eskimo a man might share his wife with a visiting hunting partner, but in that case the sexual relationships reinforced the bonds of kinship and friendship.

In the Family, Samantha went on, all conflicts had to be resolved by "hassling," or in Gestalt groups. Hassling sounded like a code word for face-to-face confrontation. I couldn't figure out yet what she meant by a Gestalt group.

"You can hassle or call a Gestalt any time of day," Samantha said. "That's the rule of twenty-four-hour encounter. It makes each person equally important to the whole group."

She said that all this face-to-face interaction and honest expression of emotions brought people closer together.

"There is no hierarchy," she said. "The most important part of it is that we give each other the space to change. I don't use my mind as a weapon any more. I don't have to. I wake up in the morning and know that fifty people love me."

She didn't use her mind as a weapon any more? She looked tiny and harmless, yet I could imagine her, like a cat in a corner, drawing blood with sharp-clawed putdowns. I, too, used my mind as a weapon to make critical distinctions, to impress and disarm. It startled me to think it might be possible to change something I took so deeply for granted.

"If you're all equal, then why do you call each other *Lord* and *Lady*?" someone called out.

"We decided to use titles to give each other more respect," Samantha answered. "We call the members who have been with us a long time and are really committed Lord and Lady. Newcomers don't have any titles, but once they make the decision to stay and we can see that they're starting to get it, they're called Mistress or Sir."

Inge Hoffman, a psychologist in the audience, raised an objection. "What about coercion in this group? Groups do tend to be coercive."

"That problem's been handled," Sean replied. He said that one man in the Family—Lord Byron—was recognized as the strongest person and the natural leader. But Byron wanted others to develop their own abilities, and so he had voluntarily moved out of the Family house.

Samantha asked for a volunteer from the audience for a demonstration of Gestalt therapy. A man raised his hand and she invited him to the stage. He sat down facing her. He looked like an engineering student, clean and blond. In her gown of burgundy velvet, she looked like his young fairy godmother. She asked him what he was feeling.

"I feel fine," he said.

"Fine?" she asked. "Could you describe that a little more?"

"Well, maybe a little nervous."

"Where in your body do you feel nervous?"

"Well, I feel a little shaky inside."

"Where inside?"

He put his right hand on his diaphragm. "Right about here."

"That's okay," she said, "let that feeling be there." She paused. "Would you be willing to talk to that feeling and ask it what it's about?" He frowned, then nodded. "What does it say?"

"It says I'm making a fool of myself coming up here like this."

"Oh. What's your answer?"

"No I'm not. I want to learn something."

"That's great. What does it say to that?"

"It says okay then." Samantha and the audience laughed.

As the dialogue, or perhaps the trilogue, continued, I found myself pulled in—impressed by her calm, surprised by his change. By the time the man left the stage, looking elated, I was the one who felt shaky inside, eager to volunteer. But Sean took a new tack.

"How many of you feel dissatisfied with your lives as they are?" he asked, scrutinizing us, arrayed before him in concentric half-circles spiralling up toward the back of the lecture hall. About half—perhaps a hundred—raised their hands, myself among them, and he asked us to stand.

"Okay, how many of you like what you've heard and think you want to join a commune?" Lots of hands. "You keep standing—everybody else sit down." A few dropped back in a blur of thuds and murmurs.

"Now," he grinned again, Jiminy Cricket in action. "Would you be willing to change your name? Everybody else sit down." More thuds.

"Give up all your possessions? Think carefully now. What are you really attached to—what would really hurt?" Some embarrassed laughter, more thinning of the ranks.

"And here's a big one—no more drugs. No dope, sure, but we mean no more alcohol, no cigarettes, no uppers or downers either. No drugs. How many are willing to do that?" After some hesitation, about ten more people sat down, and the room fell silent. There we were, roughly two dozen people desperate for change.

"You've got what it takes!" Sean exulted. "You don't need us, and we don't have enough room for you anyway. Start your own commune here." I peeked around. A man about my age in a white T-shirt and floppy hair a few rows down glanced back. A girl in horn-rimmed glasses coughed and looked embarrassed. A guy in a polyester sports jacket shrugged. Sean ended the session and, as the auditorium emptied in a burr of talk, a few of us moved forward to cluster around these emissaries of a new society and glean what we could.

March 28, 1970

Dear Daddy,

Thank you for the check. I will keep it in reserve. I am enclosing the "Smokey the Bear Sutra" by Gary Snyder, which you may not like, or again, you may, so let me know.

Sorry I have changed my mind so much lately. I really love California, but for now I also love being on a new trip: self-education. You see, my idea is to begin my liberal arts education all over—but out of school. To learn by doing and seeing and thinking, and by having contact with other people who are doing things and have made choices and thought about them.

To have a life ruled by material considerations is not my desire. . . . I am definitely not a hippy as we all understand that word, but you may sometimes wonder. I want my own path; and I'm finding it. I do not yet have a job for fall but it seems clear that I will get one—clear that I have made the right move—towards productivity.

Love, Margaret

Give up everything

2

The truth is everywhere . . . when you can see it.

—Baba Ram Dass,
The Only Dance There Is, Anchor Books, 1974

"Truth," then, is not only a matter of geography but of the time of day.

—Peter L. Berger, *An Invitation to Sociology:
A Humanistic Perspective,* Anchor Books, 1963

After their second workshop, late in the afternoon, Lord Sean and Lady Samantha invited me to dinner at the house where they were staying. It was a two-story Victorian, run-down and painted Landlord Green, occupied by a small collective that ran the health food store close to campus. In the kitchen, two of the resident women cooked, while Lord Sean, his arms folded across his chest, leaned against a battered oak table and explained more of the benefits of group marriage to me and another resident of the house, a thin young man.

"When I first joined the Family," Sean said, "I was hung up on physical beauty. I was only interested in the girls that were pretty." He grinned. Tangled, greasy curls stuck out over his ears, and his teeth showed slightly yellow. I wondered how successful he was in his approach to these girls. He certainly wasn't sexy. "But I gradually figured it out. Now I don't even notice, or even remember, who's pretty and who's not, because it's how I feel about the whole person that counts."

"Right on," said the young man standing by the sink. Samantha sat at the table nursing a cup of tea, listening without comment. It was hard to tell what her relationship was to Sean. They worked well together in front of an audience. In private they seemed like friends, maybe siblings, but not marriage partners.

"In the Family, we cut out the ego bullshit and get down to the real self," Sean went on. "You have to let go of all the props, all the artificial things that tell you what social role you're playing, like your business clothes and your big car and all of that, and when you're free of that, you start to get the only kind of freedom that really matters, the freedom within. You have to lose the false self to gain the real self."

He smiled at Samantha. She looked back in a neutral way and didn't return his smile. She didn't seem to feel obligated to be nice, like I did, and that impressed me. But she did pick up the theme.

"When you can be honest with yourself, and be who you really are, it makes your relationships so much easier," she said. "Other people see you as you really are. You don't have to hide."

I felt a thrill, almost like a pain.

"That sounds wonderful," I said, "But it's so scary."

She smiled at me.

"It depends on what you want," she said. "If you're really committed to change, you can get over the fear. Everybody has that." Her unexpected encouragement warmed me. I imagined a place in which there was enough love to go around, and yet enough freedom to be oneself—whatever that might be—wild and silly, even angry or selfish or mean.

In college, I loved the way my friends and I became wonderfully honest at late-night parties when we were drunk. I'll always remember a party in the campus Arboretum, when my friend Jean climbed a tree and stood on a limb overhanging the rest of us, who were tumbled together on blankets amid bottles of wine and leftover pizza. A Coleman lantern threw dim light on the ground. Someone spotlighted Jean with a flashlight.

"Tom!" she yelled down to a shy boy she'd had her eye on for weeks. She had the voice of a muleskinner. "I want to kiss you! Whaddya think of that?" Tom looked up with a mixture of horror and delight.

"I like it," he yelled back.

"Then why do you pretend you don't notice me?"

"I don't know!" Tom reflected, setting down a slice of pizza. "I'm sure noticing you now!"

Jean danced along her tree limb, wagging her bottom, to drunken cheers from below.

"Come on down here!" Tom jumped up and clambered over bodies to the base of the tree. Jean fell, literally, into his arms.

"Why can't we all be like that in the daytime?" I asked my friends. "Let's make a pact—to be honest and even show affection without having to get drunk."

That was 1961. Carleton College still had rules requiring girls to wear skirts in the dining room and the library; three feet on the floor during Sunday visiting hours when boys were allowed in the girls' dormitories; and other restrictions I've mercifully forgotten that expressed the college's role *in loco parentis*. Hypocrisy powered the system; girls who sat in meetings with the Dean of Women, knitting and condemning the immoral behavior of others, were known to have screwed behind the couch in the parlor or to have done other deliciously shocking things they never got caught at—while those who protested the rules or publicly broke them took the heat.

When you're slightly paranoid, as I was—never too sure I understood what was going on beneath the surface—hypocrisy can be so disturbing. Polite fictions send you off into the social wilderness with a cruelly inaccurate map. To me, reality was always more comforting than a pretty lie, but I felt alone in that preference. The Family seemed to offer a less civil alternative to straight society that would be, in its honesty, more civilized.

"In the Family, we're all just men and women," Lord Sean was saying, "brothers, sisters, mothers, fathers, husbands, wives. We lose the boundaries but we gain something much bigger."

"We do lose some freedom," Samantha said, "because our actions are for the needs of the group. It's not do your own thing—it's do what needs to be done. But that way we all benefit much more than if we were individual and separate."

Sean and Samantha seemed to be describing a return to the simplicity that served human beings well for most of our past. I had read about "primitive" societies based on cooperation instead of competition and had begun to question the whole idea that we were advanced and they were behind.

As the women were putting dinner on the table—lentil stew, salad, homemade bread—another member of the commune, Lord Arthur, walked in. He took a vacant chair next to me. He was good-looking in a boyish way, with rosy cheeks, pale skin, and relatively short, dark hair, combed and parted on one side. He wore a dark leather jacket and looked self-contained and hip. I would've felt shy around him if it weren't for his own shy smile as he sat down. He introduced himself and told me he had come up from Taos with Sean and Samantha but didn't like to speak in front of crowds.

"This afternoon I took a hike up above the Flatirons," he said. "Saw a snake and a couple of hawks. It was really beautiful."

"I love that hike," I said. He smiled again and we fell silent.

The conversation returned to the value of loss of self within the group. Arthur said he had recently read a Sufi story, and would tell it. At the word *Sufi*, all eyes turned to him. Arthur flushed, but continued in a firm voice.

"A student knocks on the teacher's door.

'Who is it?' asks the teacher.

'It's me.'

There's no answer. The student goes away. He comes back and knocks again.

'Who is it?'

'It's you.'

The teacher says 'Come in.'"

One of the women exchanged knowing smiles with the thin young man. Sean chuckled. I found this, like most Sufi stories I had heard, puzzling. Arthur, on the other hand, had my full attention.

After dinner a spontaneous jam session suddenly organized itself. The local group had drums and flutes, and it turned out that Arthur was a drummer, a professional musician in the Bay Area before he joined the

Family. The girls threw themselves into the music and danced, long skirts and scarves whirling, while Sean sat on the old green sofa reading a book. Samantha pulled me up from the sofa and I, too, allowed the drums to move me until I forgot anyone might be watching. After a while I flopped down beside Sean to catch my breath. I told him I wanted to join the Family.

"Yeah, of course you do," he said. "Everybody does." The table lamp next to me cast round balls of light on his thick glasses. His grin was impenetrable.

"No, but I mean it. I really do."

"It would be hard for you. Our place is really crowded. You'd have to give up everything."

I pictured a house something like this one, old and funky but full of color and life. Calm, spiritual men and women cooked and worked together, hugged, talked quietly. Children played in the sun. The vast Southwest sky pulsed above them. God was everywhere.

"I don't have much to give up," I said. I strained to see Sean's eyes behind his glasses. The more he discouraged me the more I felt my own need. I didn't see anything in my life in Boulder or those of my friends to hold me there. I didn't see any particular future or anything to guide me. I did have a boyfriend at the time; Tom was gentle and kind, but he was also using cocaine and I saw him increasingly giving his life up to the blaze of the drug. And I still missed Jeffrey, back in Seattle with the girlfriend who replaced me. One recent evening as I crouched in the kitchen to light the broiler and called to Tom in the living room about something or other—did he want a glass of wine—a wave of grief swept over me and I sat down on the kitchen floor and cried. Tracy Nelson's rendition of "Down So Low" was one of my favorite songs, which I played over and over.

"I've been looking for the next move anyway," I told Sean.

The World Affairs Conference had offered an intriguing side road at the moment I was contemplating getting back on the academic highway and not liking it a bit. I had even applied for a professional job, a research assistantship with an alcoholism study in Denver. It looked as though I would get it, and the closer that moment came, the worse I felt. The study involved a survey questionnaire, and my role would be to apply some cultural analysis to the answers. Contemplating it, I felt trapped.

Something about conventional research depressed me. The appeal of anthropology lay more in the art of it, the "qualitative" fieldwork involving interviewing and participant observation. I didn't believe in the objectivity of science; "objective" was just another point of view. Quantifying human responses to ambiguous questions seemed to suck all the life out of human experience.

Part of the application for the job was a question about my motivation for doing science. I found myself writing a passionate mini-essay about research. By turning subjects into objects we harm ourselves, I said, referring to Martin Buber and the sense I had drawn from his work that it is far better to maintain an "I-Thou" relation to most of the world than to dwell in the "I-It." It would be possible to find out anything we wanted to know, I said, without hurting or killing other animals, if scientists simply ruled out causing pain or killing as part of their technique. And they would do that if they stayed in touch with their feelings instead of training themselves to disengage from the subject, even when the subject is a person or another living thing.

"Well, think about it," Sean said. "You've got a couple more days."

I went home that night churning with excitement and determined to leave Boulder for Taos at the end of the week. I had recently moved into an upstairs apartment to share with Nancy, a fellow waitress at Fred's. She had an easy, lilting laugh and an easy attitude toward life, and she wasn't upset at the thought that I might take off.

"Don't worry about me," she said, "I can find another roommate. But are you sure this is what you want?"

Nancy's good nature and mothering held together a group of four of us at Fred's: besides Nancy and me, there were Hallie, married with one small daughter, and Helena, single with two small children and a boyfriend who dealt drugs and gave her a lot of grief. I would miss them. But I knew I could always come back, too. I said goodbye to the gang at Fred's.

Saturday morning, Sean, Samantha and Arthur came to pick me up in the Family's white Chevy van, which a fourth member, Lord Thomas, had driven from Taos the night before. Thomas, a redhead, was big and handsome and had an air of competence. The Family certainly had some good-looking men. Nancy followed us out to the curb in her bathrobe and stood there, a rounded figure in green chenille, her hair gold-red in the morning light of Boulder. We hugged each other and she wished me good luck. I climbed in between Arthur and Samantha and sat in silence as the van pulled away and the wooden houses and muted colors of town gave way to the open prairie. Samantha wriggled around, balled up a jacket against the window, leaned her head on it and closed her eyes.

Thomas drove south along the eastern edge of the Rockies, the prairie on the east slowly flattening out into the infinitely varied, soft colors of sky and sagebrush. The landscape itself stirred my hopes of finding home. A romantic vision of the Southwest and especially New Mexico had colored my family's experience since before I was born. My father's younger sister, Marion, had attended the University of New Mexico in the 1930s for a degree in archeology and then stayed to work at a museum in Santa Fe. New Mexico was a life-changing and life-expanding landscape for my aunt, and some of that passion was communicated to me throughout my childhood and adolescence. My parents visited Santa Fe on their honeymoon trip and bought Navajo rugs that became part of my family heritage. San Ildefonso black pottery and prints and watercolors by Pueblo and Cheyenne artists were some of the sacred objects we managed to hang onto throughout all our moves between Michigan and California. I loved most dearly an image that hung in every house we lived in: a print by the San Ildefonso Pueblo artist Awa Tsireh, showing a black bear reaching for a cluster of berries under a magical, fluted sky. I was convinced that artists and Indians, mysteries and magic lived in Taos.

We stopped in Colorado Springs for lunch and reached Taos in the late afternoon. The group lived about ten miles past town in a neighborhood called Llano Quemado, in a five-room adobe house that sat at the end of a steep side road. Winter-flat fields of dry earth stretched out around it, enclosed by ragged fences. Two yellow school buses hunched out back.

As we walked toward the house, quiet in the afternoon sun, a dark-haired woman came out to greet us. Sean introduced me as "our new member." Lady Maya smiled and took my hand. She was the essence of femininity, a little older than me, with long wavy hair, soft features, large dark eyes, and a full figure nicely draped in blue-green cotton. I felt awkward and masculine by comparison. "What's your sign?" she asked. "Leo," I said, then blurted, "Please don't reject me."

She led me inside. Fifty-five people lived in that house, yet it had a kind of empty, earthy feel, with whitewashed adobe walls and bare wooden floors worn grey with dirt and age. It smelled faintly of incense, oatmeal, sage, and dust. Afternoon sunlight shone through the open back door. The temperature in the house was about the same as outside—cool. At the entrance you could turn right to go into the kitchen or left to the small living room. The only furniture in the living room was a pile of twin mattresses used as a couch.

Three small bedrooms branched out in the back of the house—the White room, the Yellow room, the Green room. Bunkbeds lined the first two, while the Green room had four double beds on wooden frames and a couple of bookcases. The effect was Spartan—no bedspreads, just a motley collection of pillows and blankets spread up without much attention to detail. Shirts and blouses and blue jeans hung on pegs in the scarce patches of free wall.

The beds, Maya said, belonged to the women. "A man who wants to sleep in a bed has to ask permission or be invited," she informed me. I wondered if I would have a bed.

"The house is kind of full right now. You'll probably have to sleep in the living room."

Maya took me into the Green Room in back of the kitchen and introduced me to Mistress Laura, a small woman with long dark hair, who posed casually with a baby astraddle her hip. Something in her expression suggested a ferret, despite her round, pretty features. Lady Heather, a lanky dishwater blonde, set the *I Ching* aside and looked up.

"Sean told us about you," she said, without any indication of what he might have said or how she felt about it. She glanced at my suitcase. "Here, you can put that under my bed." I shoved my suitcase under the side of the wooden bed, tensing at the noise it made scraping over the floor. My Swedish stepmother had given me that suitcase for Christmas. That noise would have set her to shuddering and twitching her hands.

Laura examined my sleeping bag (also a gift from Elvera). "Oh, is it down? Far out!" she gave the baby to Heather, stroked the shiny bright blue nylon and squeezed to gauge the thickness of the down. "This would be great out in the bus. It gets cold out there."

I was aware of the rule of giving up one's possessions and was eager to show that I was not unduly attached to this thing, although I was actually very attached. I had brought so little with me—only the essentials: one small suitcase, a tape recorder, a camera, a knapsack, and this sleeping bag. It was well-made, of high quality goosedown, and had cost about $200. I couldn't have afforded to buy it myself.

"Oh, sure, take it," I said, and watched it leave the room on Laura's other hip. Heather went back to her reading. Maya faded away with a faint, motherly smile. I felt set adrift, a sea creature caught in the tide. What was I supposed to do? Sean and Samantha had disappeared into other parts of the house as soon as we arrived. Arthur and Thomas, too, a hug, a smile, and they were absorbed into the weightless honeycomb of the tribe.

A man creates reality

3 *When you bite your fingernails, you're eating the Buddha . . . .*
— Baba Ram Dass

In early evening, about twenty of us sat outside on boxes and tree stumps, eating spaghetti, garlic bread, and an iceberg lettuce salad. There was a communal pitcher of water, and after I had poured some into a glass for myself, I realized that others just picked it up and swigged from it. I recognized this as an opportunity to suspend my middle-class standards of hygiene. I thought of a favorite essay by British social anthropologist Mary Douglas, in which she said that "dirt is merely matter out of place." Cleanliness, dirt—all those things are culturally relative. The water tasted good.

The cool air smelled of sage. The Sangre de Cristo peaks rose dark in the east; the last light silhouetted low hills on the west side of the valley, across the Rio Grande. A barbed wire fence defined the large, unused field that belonged to this house. The neighboring house on the left was tucked behind a grove of cottonwood trees with huge ghostly trunks and a few new leaves. A curve of the ridge behind us hid the house on the right. A truck rattled by on the dirt road. The only other sounds were our voices.

Most of the group members sitting there were young—in their early twenties—and white. Two women were pregnant. There were three babies, two toddlers, and a four year old. They were mostly pale-skinned, even pasty-faced, with straggling hair and ill-fitting clothes. These didn't look like the healthy, vibrant, self-realized folks I had expected. The desultory conversation didn't interest me; it seemed to consist mostly of "far out," "groovy," "hang," "flow," and "man."

After dinner I wandered into the living room, a space no bigger than a pause between kitchen and bedroom. A large black man sat on the stacked mattresses that served as the couch, leaning against the wall with his arms folded across his chest. He glanced at me and all I saw was a dark, closed face, hooded eyes, a sullen lip. He wore loose pants and a white undershirt that emphasized his shoulders and biceps. I started, lowered my eyes, and wondered how to back out.

He stirred and I looked again. He wasn't smiling. He looked hostile and bored. He looked like somebody who would never like me, who would hate me for being white. His face looked absolutely closed. Without any polite, helpful clues I felt trapped.

"What's the matter?" he asked.

"I'm afraid of you," I said. His eyebrows jumped and his eyes widened a bit on that.

"Afraid of me? What for?"

"I don't know what you're thinking."

"I'm not thinking anything." He shifted around, jostling the mattresses. His voice sounded muffled. "I'm wishing somebody would come up and tell me welcome home. I'm tired when I come back to the pad."

"Huh."

"Come closer," Noah said. I stepped up near him. His face softened. He straightened out his legs, leaned over and took my hands.

"Where you from?"

"I've been living in Boulder."

"You've been living in Boulder? Where you from? Where do your folks live?"

"My mother lives in Palm Springs. My father and stepmother live in L.A."

"Oh yeah? Far out. I used to live in L.A." Noah pulled me closer. I stood between his knees looking into his eyes—big, kind, deep brown eyes. He had a high, flat-top, conked hairdo and a Trotskyesque beard around his chin. He looked about my age, maybe a few years older.

"When I was fifteen, I was living with prostitutes in LA, and they used to take me with them to the nightclubs." (I tried to imagine this life. When I was fifteen, I was a senior at Redlands High School and passing notes in Latin class.)

"Yeah, when I was nineteen I got caught twice for armed robbery. Then when I got out of the pen, I was twenty-three, and I was a felon.

"Somehow I knew I was good for something," he said, "but I never knew what until I met up with Byron and Daniel and joined the Family."

He smiled and his eyes lit up and I saw his white, straight teeth. His cheekbones and forehead shone with yellow-gold highlights.

"The Family's all I have," Noah concluded.

By 10 p.m. Noah and I were sitting side by side on the edge of the kitchen table, dangling our feet, as naked bodies—girls, babies, men— sorted themselves out between kitchen, bathroom, and bed. The Family ebb and flow filled the Green Room, which we faced. Inside, a muted light under a paper shade threw shadows up the bookcase stacked with paperbacks and copies of the *I Ching*, the Bible, the Book of Rosicrucians. A long stick of incense anchored between two books dropped its soft trail of ashes and raised a fine column of smoke.

Despite the traffic through it, the Green room seemed like a private club. Daniel, a golden-skinned man who looked like he might be part southeast Asian or Filipino, sat beside his solemn partner, Isabel, on one of the double beds. She held a dark-haired baby on her lap. They turned to look into each other's eyes as if they were conversing without words. Leanne, a thin, flat-chested brunette, stripped meditatively, put on a short cotton nightgown, and climbed into the bed across from them. Arthur, on the farthest bed next to the bathroom door, still looking streetwise in jeans and leather jacket, called softly to Daniel as if to tell him a private joke. Gretchen, in her underpants, turned her back to us and strolled toward the bathroom as Jennifer, humming, left it and moved through the room towards us, her freckled thighs, belly, and small breasts in motion.

Richard came into the kitchen from the other direction, probably from the outhouse, naked except for the luxuriant dark hair carpeting his chest, arms, and crotch. A young Marlon Brando. I tried to keep my eyes on his face. His smile was sweet and unpretentious, as if he weren't aware he was handsome. He met Noah's eyes, reached out for a welcoming handclasp, murmured, "Welcome back, brother," and went on into the White room.

I slid down off the kitchen table and fished my toothbrush out of my purse under Heather's bed. On the bathroom shelf beside the sink was a forest of toothbrushes—perhaps fifty of them—jumbled together like pickup sticks. Too much equality for me. I used my own, and when I was done, returned it to my purse.

That night I slept on one of the mattresses on the living room floor, alongside Stanley and William. The sheets held a history of the Family, stained with body fluids and gritty as the front yard. William, a big guy with greasy chin-length hair, wore longjohns and a sad, plaid shirt. As he flopped his sheet and blankets around trying to get comfortable, his ripe body smell puffed across my face. Stanley, pasty-faced and lumpy, tucked himself in wearing light blue pajamas that made him look like a forlorn little boy.

Outside, the world was quiet; the sky was full of stars. Inside, however, the house was restless. Lights went on and off in the kitchen, doors banged, and the CB radio periodically erupted in loud static. I would have slept better alone outside in my sleeping bag; still, it was comforting to be surrounded by so many people. It was easy to put up with the dirt in exchange for this sense of being enfolded in a group of people my own age. It was more intimate and more companionable than a college dormitory, less intimate than sleeping with a lover, more like what I imagined it would be to have a lot of brothers and sisters. Though Stanley and William were not the brothers I most wanted to have, their simple human presence was comforting. At dawn I lay on my sagging mattress listening to their gentle breathing beside me and snores from the next room.

At last, I was truly dropping out. The first time I left graduate school was a cakewalk compared to this. It was as hard for me to quit graduate school as for my mother, who tried her first cigarette at sixteen, to quit smoking. She had the courage to get a divorce in the mid-1950s; perhaps that was her equivalent of dropping out.

In college, I admired the one or two boys I knew who had the courage to drop out. My friends and I resented the school's paternalism and chafed at the stupid rules, but quitting school seemed unthinkable. Where would I go? What would I do? How would I support myself? And, of course, my parents wouldn't let me. I was "only" eighteen. I completed my B.A. at nineteen and went straight to graduate school in anthropology the following fall—1964.

In the late sixties, dropping out took on a deeper meaning, as boys and young men had to decide where they stood in relation to the draft and to fighting a war in Vietnam. Dropping out could mean going to Canada to avoid the draft, or it could mean taking LSD, seeing into the heart of the universe, and choosing to reject the hypocrisy, materialism, racism, and inequality that defined the dark side of the American coin. I suppose dropping out meant all that for me, but also it meant simply a personal rebellion against everything I thought of as "straight": being good, doing what my parents or professors expected, wearing Peter Pan collars, staying on a career track, having and loving a routine. I wanted adventure and I wanted to be safe and I really didn't want to know what else I wanted.

Around seven o'clock the house started stirring, and those of us sleeping on the floor had to get up or be stepped on. We folded the sheets and piled up the mattresses so that they were once again the couch. I couldn't imagine going to the bathroom with other people using the sink or taking a shower, so I went around back to the outhouse, a three-sided shed that faced away from the house into a stand of willows. It actually smelled better than the heavily used indoor bathroom, but Stanley was already there. "It's okay," he said, as I apologized and turned away, "Here, have a seat." (It was a two-holer.) I went back in and waited for a turn at the bathroom.

While I was sorting through my suitcase looking for something to wear, Heather asked if I would be willing to put my clothes into the "cut-loose box." I said I would. Laura pounced. She pulled out a cotton blouse I happened to like a lot, an indigo jersey with a boat neck and long, graceful sleeves. It was new, and I felt that it was flattering and feminine on me. Laura pulled off her blouse and put mine on. Her bust filled it out more, and the color set off her long, dark hair. I agreed it looked great on her and that she should have it. I rummaged around in the cut-loose box and found a faded yellow shirt that wasn't too bad over my jeans.

Four or five women were bustling around in the kitchen making scrambled eggs, potatoes, and toast. They dished out portions at the stove as grownups and children fluttered through the kitchen and set- tled like moths on the scarce chairs or spilled out into the other rooms. It was William's turn to do the dishes. He ate slowly, and, when he was done, rose like a tired lumberjack, rolled up his sleeves and posed his bulk at the sink as if he faced a great challenge.

Not long after breakfast there was a stir as a car pulled up outside. "Far out, Byron's back," someone said, and Daniel and Arthur led the movement out to see him. I walked along in the backwash. Lord Byron had returned from Los Angeles with Lord George and Lord Noah the night before, but had stayed in town—a voluntary exile, as the story went, so that other members of the Family wouldn't rely on him so much. Lord Thomas, who seemed to be a trusted chauffeur—I thought of him as one of the young lieutenants—had gone to town and retrieved Lord Byron in the black Mustang. The men milled around greeting each other with hugs, shoulder slaps, and "Welcome back, man."

Samantha led me over and introduced me to Byron. He was a pow- erfully built man, but short—maybe about 5 feet 8. He was "black" only in terms of American racial politics; his color was actually like acorns or dry oak leaves. He had wispy, fine black hair receding toward the crown, a wide nose turned up at the tip like a child's, and clear hazel eyes. His smile seemed gentle and comical, partly because he had no upper front teeth, which made his lips seem curly. He looked older than the rest of us by about ten years. Lord Byron took my hand, smiled into my eyes in a way that made me feel pretty, and welcomed me. His hand was warm. I smiled back.

A pregnant woman walked by and he gazed at her with satisfaction, then turned and patted my stomach. "We should make you one of those," he said. I withdrew my hand and smiled uncertainly. Lady April, who had been moving slowly toward us like a beautiful, golden mast- head, her pregnant belly before her and long blonde hair behind, reached him and they embraced. My audience was over. It was like the love-in at

Griffith Park in Los Angeles two years before. That was the first time I had experienced this new way of being with other people, where you didn't necessarily say anything. You wandered around and when you met someone's eyes you both stopped and looked deeply at each other. Then you smiled and embraced, or spoke, or glanced away and moved on to the next encounter.

In this case, however, I stood still, fighting off swarms of critical thoughts. What was I to him, a new baby carriage? Not that I was against having a baby. (*A baby. When the time comes. With the right partner.*) What kind of a remark was that—Hello, let's get you pregnant? But he seemed very nice. My stomach hurt and I went looking for some baking soda.

Inside the house, there was nowhere to be alone. There were people everywhere—hanging out, wrapped up together, napping, reading, talking—and nowhere in particular for me. I found some baking soda in a kitchen cabinet, then a teaspoon and a glass, and as I filled the glass with water someone came up behind me and asked how I was doing. It was Samantha.

"I don't know," I said. "It's weird not to have any privacy."

"You'll get used to it." Her eyes were enormous. "You have to learn how to find privacy inside yourself. That's the only place it really is, anyway." It was true that she seemed to have found her own way. I was rarely aware of her, and yet she had been at the house all the time since we arrived. She patted my arm and added, "You'll be fine. Lady Heather likes you, and she's a boss lady." This, like Byron's remark, struck a discordant note to me. No hierarchy?

Sean bustled up like a concerned crane and asked the Family question: What was I feeling? I didn't mention my stomach.

"I don't know. I think maybe I want to go home."

He immediately called a Gestalt session. The word passed around quickly and about twenty people gathered in the Green Room, perching on the beds, sitting on the floor and leaning against the walls. Someone dragged a straight-backed chair in and put me on the "hot seat," in the middle of the open doorway. Sean was the leader of the Gestalt, and he repeated his question.

"I don't want to be a part of this," I said. "It's boring."

"So you're bored?"

"Yeah." I hoped this hadn't hurt anyone's feelings. But I went on in the silence. "There are cliques and group processes. Some people have higher status than others, that's obvious. I've seen it all before, and I don't dig it. The titles are silly. Why are all the new names English? Why is there no Juanita, no Cucamonga, everything so seriously English? And besides, there's a lot of male chauvinism."

Several people spoke up, with such agreement that it felt like a chorus: I wasn't in touch with myself, didn't know what I was really feeling, and didn't understand what was really happening.

"Women's lib is bullshit," Byron announced, to my amazement. "Real men and real women don't need it." He smiled at me again in a kindly way. "You're a real woman, too. You just don't know it yet." I saw earnest nods among the listeners.

A real woman, me? Did he mean I was sexy? Did he mean I had passion? Did he mean I could have babies, be a good mother, support my husband(s) in all their endeavors? As a teenager in Southern California I understood implicitly that, at the least, my body was inadequate to my role. My breasts would never be big enough, my thighs slender enough, my nails long enough. Never. I had to make my way in the world by being bright and pretty, but underneath there was something I lacked. Perhaps this showed on my face. Lord George offered consolation:

"Stick with us," he said, "And you'll get the self you've always wanted."

Lord Sean said that when we met in Boulder, he could see that I was "really in the Void." This startled me. I was certainly unhappy. Is that being in the Void? He leaned toward me, adjusting his glasses. "When you don't even know your own feelings, you're stuck. You can't see other people clearly, either."

I flushed. I felt like the new kid in seventh grade. Everybody but me seemed so sure of their perceptions. My stomach hurt again.

"At first I didn't like the idea of titles either," Lady Melinda said, looking soft and sleepy-eyed. She sat with her feet up on the bed, resting her back against Lord Thomas. "We started them, though, because we weren't treating each other with enough respect. If I have to say 'Lady Heather' or 'Lord Arthur,' it makes me stop and think about who that person is." There were murmurs of agreement. Thomas curved his arm

around her. I felt a pang of loneliness. But I remembered Byron's con-
descending pat on my stomach and tried again.

"I've thought a lot about male and female roles," I started out
bravely, "and I think I have something to say . . ." Thomas interrupted.

"You've just thought about it: we've lived it."

Lady Isabel and Lord Daniel, like lioness and lion, stirred. Their
bond was visible in the way each responded to the slightest movement
of the other. Over her baby's fuzzy head, she said, "I've experienced that
a man creates reality."

What on earth did she mean? A slight breeze through the doorway
made me shiver. In the ensuing silence, Leanne, who had been listening
with her eyes downcast and an inward, mournful look, spoke up.

"The Family is all I have," she said, in an accent I interpreted as
English working class. "I was nothink without the Family."

"There's nowhere else for me to go," William said. Others nodded.
Sean opened his arms to include us all and said, as if reciting a mantra,
"We are the dropouts, the misfits, but together we can become much
more."

Isabel spoke quietly, but everyone listened. "We don't want to keep
you here if you don't want to stay. You don't understand what's going on
yet, and you can't if you don't stay longer. Why don't you wait a while
and see? Open your mind to us. Learn what we have to give you."

I had no answer to this. The group fell silent. A few slipped away to
start fixing lunch, and it was clear that the meeting had ended. I wandered out into the yard. Lord Byron asked me how I was doing.

"I'm pretty confused," I said. He patted my shoulder.

"You *should* be totally confused by now."

He went off toward the school buses. I sat on a wooden box and
chewed a couple of fingernails. A piece of cuticle was loose on the side
of my middle finger, the place where holding a pen formed a callus. I
got it between my front teeth and tugged a little; it felt like it would pull
loose without drawing blood, so I tugged harder and a small strip of dead
skin gave way. One more pull, though, and a twinge of pain and a drop
of blood let me know I had gone too far.

A soft wind scattered grains of sand across the yard and stirred the
fragrance of sagebrush. A redtailed hawk lifted off a telephone pole on
the far side of the field. I watched its wings flex and straighten and flex

again as it rose, banked, and set off on a mission like a jet with a clear flight plan and good communication with the tower. I sucked the side of my finger and searched my pockets for a Kleenex to wrap around it to absorb the blood.

Follow the flow

4

The heart thinks constantly. This cannot be changed, but the movements of the heart—that is, a man's thoughts—should restrict themselves to the immediate situation. All thinking that goes beyond this only makes the heart sore.

—*I Ching*, Chapter 52. *Ken*/Keeping Still, Mountain

The naked cottonwood trees on the far side of the field thrust up their arms as if pleading for leaves. April here seemed a crisp study in black, brown, and pewter, so perfectly opposite to spring in the Northwest. I wandered across the field sorting through my alternatives. The air right now in Seattle would sag with moisture. It was probably one of those days when you couldn't remember if it rained or not because the ground was so wet and the sky so uniformly grey that it didn't matter.

The day I first entered the production studio of KRAB-FM, Seattle's first "alternative" radio station, it seemed like it had been raining for about six months. It was Valentine's Day, 1968, and I was answering an on-air call for volunteers. I hadn't had a date in a long time, or even coffee with a friend, for that matter, and my apartment was small and dark. Out of self-destructive caprice I had decided to write a master's thesis on a subject I knew nothing about with an advisor I couldn't stand. In short, I was lonely and depressed.

The radio station broadcast from a former donut shop, a shack with one twelve-by-twelve room lined with records and tapes and an even smaller "control room" or studio that held the microphone, turntable, and tape decks. The budget came from listener subscriptions and founder Lorenzo Milam's inherited wealth.

I loved the varied and sometimes uncertain voices that announced the programs on KRAB, and the unpredictability of it, the occasional silences, the world music, the unusual talk. It never played top 40 tunes or abbreviated news bits delivered staccato. The pleas for money could be silly or pathetic, but the calls for volunteers sounded friendly.

The donut shop smelled of musty cardboard and stale cigarettes. Windows on the front wall let in a little bit of watery grey light. Lorenzo himself, a husky man with curly brown hair and glasses, sat in the glow of a desk lamp at the back of the room. The record library towered behind him, and he faced the window into the control room, where another man in headphones sat by a microphone and turntable reading a book. Classical music—Mozart, perhaps—came from speakers high on the walls. Lorenzo didn't get up to greet me, and I didn't notice until later the crutches that leaned against the wall.

I said I had heard KRAB was looking for volunteers.

"Yep, we are," he said, leaning back. "We need good announcers. What are you interested in?"

"Interested? I'm in graduate school in anthropology. I'm interested in everything."

"Perfect." He chuckled.

"But I thought I'd like to do a program of classical music of India."

"Do you know anything about Indian music?" he asked.

"Not much, but I was in India my junior year of college and that's where I discovered I liked it. At least I can pronounce the names."

I told him about hearing Ravi Shankar for the first time in Banaras, the ancient city on the banks of the Ganges, at the All-India Music

Festival. The festival went on all night in a big tent. It was mid-winter, and in North India the winter can get cold.

"Ravi Shankar came on at three in the morning, and most of the audience had been there since afternoon, coming and going, feeding babies, eating snacks. It was more informal and personal than an American concert; the musicians made a lot of eye contact with the audience. People around me were keeping time with their hands and moving with the beat. The tabla player was a master, too, Chatur Lal."

Lorenzo nodded as if he had heard of Chatur Lal.

The musicians competed with each other, the sitar playing a long complicated passage and then the tabla mimicking it in rhythm and tone. As the music built to a climax, my whole body swayed to the beat, and I realized that everyone around me, the whole audience, was rocking, transported, keeping time with the musicians. The tabla shattered into a million perfectly timed pieces and the sitar answered in notes.

"They played until dawn," I concluded, "and afterwards we walked out into the street and the whole sky was violet and pink, and we could see the spires of the Golden Temple outlined against it."

"Fantastic," Lorenzo said. "We *need* a program of Indian music. Could you do two hours a week?"

He waved a hand at the records behind him and said I would find a large collection right there. And maybe I had some others?

"Oh, yes, I have lots."

"Good on ya."

He gripped the arms of his chair and raised himself up, wrestled his crutches into position, and hitched and swayed to the door of the control room with a skill reminiscent of dancing. He introduced me to the announcer, Jeffrey, who stubbed out a cigarette in a quick movement, slipped off his headphones and stood up to shake my hand.

As our eyes met I felt a shiver of attraction. Jeffrey had wide shoulders and I measured myself against them. His wide-set eyes, aquiline nose and sensuous mouth contrasted with the dark curly hair that framed his face as softly as a girl's. He had a sweet smile.

Lorenzo told him about my new program.

"Great! When can you start?"

"Soon," I said. I noticed that the tonearm had a splint—a matchstick attached with a rubber band. "Why's that?"

Jeffrey giggled. "To balance it, of course."

I loved his voice, deep but moderated by some kind of self-depre-cation, a tendency to glance down when he spoke, a twist of his head.

"You'll have to take a test to get a third-class broadcaster's license," Jeffrey said. "In the meantime, someone else will engineer for you." We settled on Thursday nights at 8 for my program. He gave me a booklet to study for the third-class license. His hand brushed mine and I felt a little curl of delight.

When I arrived at the station the next Thursday to start my pro-gram, Jeffrey was there to engineer for me. I pulled a Folkways collec-tion of tribal music out of the archives to supplement some of my own favorites for the first program: North Indian flute, Bengali bhajans (devotional songs), Ravi Shankar playing Raga Bhairavi.

We both crammed into the studio. He unplugged and reconnected a forest of black cables on the back of the control board to set up the tape recorders and turntable for broadcast. He gave me some head-phones and adjusted the microphone close to my lips. I practiced speak-ing into it and hearing myself in my ears. He sat next to the control board and across from me, almost knee-to-knee, at a second microphone.

The evening commentary was finishing up on a large tape recorder. KRAB aired commentaries daily; virtually anybody could come up to the station and record a 15-minute commentary, if Lorenzo thought they were interesting. And they were interesting: "ordinary" citizens with political views, housewives, architects, activists, oddballs. Tonight it was Flo Ware, a local activist who had founded a parents' organization.

"Don't try to talk to all the people you think are out there," Jeffrey said. "That'll make you nervous, and you'll sound too formal. Just talk to me."

As the commentary concluded—"This is Flo Ware, tellin' you good night and God bless you"—KRAB's trademark silence fell and I looked at Jeffrey. Jeffrey smiled, flipped a switch, and spoke softly into the microphone: "This is KRAB-FM. We have Margaret Hollenbach here with—with what?"

"With classical music of India," I said, and heard my own voice, oddly breathy, answering his. I had the flute selection cued up on the turntable. Jeffrey flipped more switches to turn off the microphones. I noticed his hands; talented hands, I thought. What was it about them? . . . Slender fingers, well-defined tendons, something about how he used them, quick gestures, flashes of light. The black vinyl disk turned. The slow cry of the flute spiralled out. Jeffrey smiled again.

"You did great."

"I'm shaking."

"That's okay—you'll get over it. It's okay to sound human."

At quarter of 10 I cued up the last piece, a threshing song from a tribal region of Orissa, announced it, and took off my headphones.

"How're you getting home?" he asked.

"The bus."

"Want a ride?"

"Sure, thanks."

The late-night announcer arrived, a gangly redhead in plaid shirt and blue jeans, smiling and apologizing for taking up space. Whatever his default opinion of himself, KRAB welcomed him; he had skills. He could keep the station on the air, play strange music, talk other lonely people through to morning.

Jeffrey's car was a beater, an old Chevy. He ground the gears, laughed, reached for my hand. In the dark I could see the outline of his face and hair, feel the warmth of his hand. I slid closer and he put his arm around me, asked me to shift into third, then downshift going up Capital Hill. The car roared up the hill. My apartment at the time was a walkup in an old house. I didn't ask him in, but something about him seemed inevitable; I felt reluctant to move away from him. I nosed his neck. He smelled good. No soap, no sweat, just warm man skin. He touched my cheek—that gave me shivers. We kissed. My heart was pounding. I jumped out of the car and ran up the porch and let myself in without looking back.

Jeffrey called the next day and invited me over for dinner. He lived in the basement of an architect's house and cooked on a two-burner hot plate. I was impressed that he would cook for me, impressed at the elegance of his poverty. A green porcelain table lamp softened the edges of his nearly empty living-dining-cooking room. We sat at an old wooden table, on straight-backed chairs that squeaked. The art posters on the wall were by artists unfamiliar to me: Redon, Kokoschka, something abstract and incomprehensible. He said his favorite composer was Monteverdi. I wasn't sure I had ever heard Monteverdi. KRAB was playing Elly

Ameling singing Schubert *lieder* that night, though, and I thought I understood Schubert.

"What do you like about Schubert?" he asked.

"His music is so passionate, so sad," I said.

"I like Monteverdi because it *isn't* sad," he said.

Some photographs lay on the bookshelf, and I picked up one because it looked like India. A beige cow walked along an unpaved street littered with garbage—banana peels, leaves, papers—and blotched with mud puddles. Sanskritic graffiti in red paint crawled across a wooden fence.

"Ugh, I remember that so vividly," I said. "The dirt, the poverty."

"But this isn't a picture of poverty," Jeffrey said. "Look at it. It's just a beautiful pattern of light and dark. I'm looking at the form, not the content."

"But you *should* look at the content."

"Why?"

"Because there's suffering there. People get sick from dirt. That cow is starving—its ribs look like sticks. And that graffiti is a political slogan. Probably telling the government to feed its people."

"I'm not interested in should," he said. "I'm interested in color and light. To an artist, good and bad aren't the point. Morality gets in the way of your perception. Play around with it—look at what is."

I tried to imagine someone who could get out from under the monumental Should that ran my life, and the lives of most of the people I knew, especially graduate students. One should study, one should excel, one should do something useful, one should be nice, one should. . . . What kind of a life would emerge out of a greater attention to Is?

"That's kind of scary," I said, but I liked him even more.

We didn't go to bed that night. I had a half-conscious rule not to have sex until the third date.

I began hanging out at the station. I was still nominally in graduate school, but my center of gravity shifted to life outside the university, to the artists, writers, and weirdos who populated KRAB. Jeffrey and I had our third date. He invited me to go with him to dinner at Lorenzo's houseboat, and we became a couple in Lorenzo's orbit. When we decided to live together, we rented a room at the Jean Paul Sartre No Exit Rooming House. The owner and manager was Richard A. C. Greene, a smooth, round man of discreet and mysterious sexuality who later gained some fame when he ran for Washington State Land Commissioner on a tongue-in-cheek platform he and Lorenzo wrote. The one campaign promise I remember regarded Indian fishing rights, a big controversy in Washington in the years before the Boldt decision granted Indians half of the catch of salmon as part of their treaty rights. Richard said he would throw back any Indians under 5'5".

Lorenzo retired from KRAB and chose Jeffrey as the first post-Lorenzo station manager. Jeffrey hired me as program director and I dropped out of graduate school to work full-time at KRAB. Lorenzo's principle, which we carried on, was to air programs, ideas, and music that couldn't be heard anywhere else. We aired firebrand talks by Southern Christian Leadership Conference minister James Bevel; local panel discussions; commentaries; Japanese Gagaku (court music); South Indian flute; Argentine guitarist Atahualpa Yupanqui; midnight rock 'n' roll.

A listener-supported, accessible radio station has a power, a sweet power, that appeals to many who have never before felt heard. KRAB was unconditional love. Once you were accepted as a person with either a talent or a skill to contribute, you had a place to hang out, an astonishing sound library to browse in, and permission to test the limits of what you could do. Our announcers got a time slot and a program name and then it was all up to them. Listeners could call in and talk immediately to a human. A community was created in the lovemaking between listener and player.

KRAB became my dearest love, and Jeffrey a close second. Jeffrey and I would sit at home listening to the radio and say, "Ah, there's John Cunnick . . . he's good." Or we would hear somebody playing something tacky and pick up the phone to lecture them about taste. Being program director pulled together all the scattered pieces of my life. It allowed me to use my knowledge and curiosity about everything to find or create programs that made the whole world come alive.

The power went to my head. One Sunday I was alone upstairs in the rooming house, looking out over the trees to the blue sky, and I wanted to hear Swami Parvatikar, a wandering yogi in South India, play his traditional, devotional music on the svaramandala, a South Indian cymbalom. I picked up the phone, called the station, talked to the announcer,

37

and in a few minutes there it was—coming out of the speakers in my room. Let there be Swami Parvatikar.

Jeffrey liked performance art, which sometimes made for weird radio. There was a long-running weekly series by Paul Sawyer, a Unitarian minister, of recordings of daily life in his house. He would keep the tape recorder on in the living room while he read silently. Background noise, occasional turning pages, a sigh, a belch, the couchsprings squeaking.

This was a happy, creative time in Seattle. Tom Robbins was working on his first book, *Another Roadside Attraction*, and writing wonderful, sophisticated movie reviews for *Seattle* magazine. Richard Brautigan's *In Watermelon Sugar* had just come out, and its gentle, surreal humor embodied the subculture perfectly. Lots of artists and writers lived in or near the city and partied in the fertile, green rain. KRAB and the underground newspaper, the *Helix*, co-sponsored the Piano Drop, another iconic event. Thousands of people paid a dollar each to gather in a field somewhere east of Seattle on a warm spring day to watch (and hear) a helicopter drop a grand piano onto a pile of lumber. As described in detail in Walt Crowley's *Rites of Passage: A Memoir of the Sixties in Seattle*, the piano missed its mark and dropped without a note onto soft ground instead. Nevertheless, it was a great party.

One night Jeffrey didn't come home until sometime after midnight. He looked like someone adrift on a raft in the Bering Sea, cold and unreachable, and went to bed without any explanation. In the morning when I went out to my car, I found blood spattered all over the steering wheel and the windshield and even up on the sun visor. Jeffrey was subject to nosebleeds, but this was incredible. I asked him what happened. He said he had decided to drop in on his ex-wife around midnight.

"She opened the door with a big grin, holding her toothbrush, wearing a blouse and nothing else," he told me. "She was expecting somebody else."

While he was sitting outside in my car thinking about it, his nose exploded.

Jeffrey reminisced so much about his ex-wife's beautiful breasts, her good nature, and so on, that I was convinced I was hopelessly inadequate and he would inevitably get back together with her.

One night we were arguing and driving through the rain in my old white Volvo. I felt an enormous pressure in my head, my heart; he was tormenting me; he would never love me; he would always prefer his ex-wife. I grabbed the door handle and tried to open it and jump out. He reached across me and held onto the door handle, then stopped on the side of the road. I flailed at him, twisting and struggling across the gear shift in the floor between us.

"Why me?" I howled.

"Because I choose you," he answered. I quit struggling and he let go of my arms. I felt such a yearning toward him, toward his warmth and his talent. Did he mean he loved me, loved a softness in me, and I loved him, and his hands, so much like my small hands, and I pressed my face into his hands and kissed their warm dark palms, and we held each other on the side of the road in the dark.

But sometimes I felt so angry. I couldn't say exactly at what. I would get complicated and weepy. "What is this about?" Jeffrey asked. I said I didn't know. I said I thought it was better to get mad at myself than at him.

"No, I can take it," he said. "It scares me to see it dorking around inside of you. I don't know when it will explode and splatter on me."

Jeffrey resigned as station manager. He was an artist, not by nature an administrator, and the horrendous press of details did him in. He quit abruptly one day, leaving a note in the typewriter that said, "My head is a cantaloupe being picked apart by crows."

Living at the rooming house was getting to be a hassle. Richard had a snake-eyed, nasty-faced lover he frequently left in charge, and the vibes changed from genial to unpleasant when Richard wasn't around. He knew it himself. He said he had "left a viper to guard his pit." Jeffrey found a house to rent, where he would have enough room to paint. He hadn't asked me to share in the choice of the house but expected me to move in with him. The traffic noise, even late at night, tormented me but didn't bother him. I decided not to move in. I rented a one-room basement apartment on an alley on Capital Hill. He interpreted this act of self-protection as a betrayal and implied that he had left his wife for less.

Jeffrey showed me what he had been working on—small abstract compositions with a lot of white space and sparse color. I have never understood abstract art, and I couldn't find much to connect to in these paintings. I said something to that effect.

"Well, if you don't like my art, you don't like me," he said.

"But I do like you. I just don't understand abstract art." He frowned and turned away.

As far as he was concerned, I had broken up with him. I thought we were just taking a breather, and we would look for a house we could both be comfortable in. But two weeks later, when I asked if we could meet and talk, he revealed that he already had another girlfriend. She was pretty, he said, and only seventeen.

In the meantime, KRAB's Board of Directors, a capricious collection of professors and artists, hired a talented nineteen-year-old volunteer to replace Jeffrey as station manager. Chuck was a better manager and more interested in politics than Jeffrey. Under his tenure the programs ventured further into left-wing politics and particularly into criticism of the war in Vietnam. He was easy to work with and we agreed on the politics.

Chuck applied for status as a conscientious objector and agonized over whether he would go to Canada if his application was turned down. On the day of one of his many appearances before a judge to establish his pacifism, Chuck didn't come into work until early afternoon. He was telling me and Hank, a volunteer, about his court hearing, when a well-dressed, middle-aged man walked in, said he was the FCC inspector, and told us that he was taking the station off the air; the FCC (Federal Communications Commission) had received several calls complaining that we were airing obscenities. Chuck and I stared at each other and both realized at the same time that we had turned the broadcast monitor off while discussing his situation. We knew the current program was a speech by Southern Christian Leadership Conference minister James Bevel, and that Bevel did tend to pepper his speech with obscenities. But the volunteer had edited the swear words out. Hadn't he? We turned to Hank.

"Yeah, I edited the tape last night," he mumbled. Hank rarely spoke up or made eye contact. I turned up the monitor. There was Bevel, perceptive, charismatic, foul-mouthed, and intact.

"How could you do this?" I yelled at Hank. "The words are all in there! Whaddyou mean you edited it?"

"I did. I took the half-track machine home and worked on it there. I cut them all out. I erased them and inserted the beeps."

Chuck went to the control room to take the program off and announce that the FCC required that the station shut down. The FCC inspector stood near the door, looking a little apologetic.

"Oh shit, I get it," I moaned. "We put it on the air on the full-track machine. It's playing the part you didn't delete." Hank, without looking at me, nodded. "You didn't label it half-track edited." He looked up briefly. Gloom descended.

The station went off the air for a couple of weeks while the Board of Directors figured out how to respond to the FCC. We continued working, catching up with paperwork, tidying the archives, explaining the situation to callers and volunteers. One evening I worked late on a music program, absorbed in choosing records and listening to tapes. It was February, almost exactly a year since I first volunteered. I locked up the donut shop and caught a Roosevelt bus to a transfer point in the University District. I had to wait a while for another bus.

The street is empty, long after rush hour. A cold rain on the cusp of snow creates blurred curtains under each street light. I huddle in my old black rabbit-fur coat, one hand picking at the fuzz on the bottom of the pocket, the other holding the front of the coat tight against me, wishing I had worn gloves, even wishing for an umbrella. Everybody's used to cold rain in Seattle; nobody bothers to carry an umbrella.

No houses remain on this block, just empty lots and businesses with their lights turned off for the night. Up the street on this side is the stereo shop. Up the street on that side the Taj Mahal Indian Restaurant—closed now. Not much business in this location. From the left, Ravenna Boulevard curves out of Ravenna Park and on the right it curves off to go under the freeway. I can see the dark boulevard of trees that form a wide center strip. I don't have a bus schedule, but I know the buses run at least every half hour until 10 o'clock.

I realize with a start that a man has come up behind me. Too close. I turn.

"Come with me," he says. "I have a gun."

He's a stocky white man in a trench coat, not much taller than me. He lifts up a brown paper bag that covers his hands to show me the gun.

"You must be kidding," I say, staring. He has a crew cut and horn-rimmed glasses. He looks about thirty. His eyes—cold eyes with small black pupils.

"No, I'm not. I have a knife, too. If I don't get you with the gun I'll get you with the knife." He grabs my arm, twists it behind me, and pushes me down the street toward the corner of Ravenna. I scream.

"Shut up or I'll kill you," he says. I stop and look straight into those eyes.

"Do you want to rape me or kill me?" I ask. The eyes flicker. He pauses.

"Rape you."

I know he will kill me.

I scream again. He yanks at my arm and pushes me forward. We jerk and scuffle about 30 feet down Roosevelt and around the corner onto Ravenna. I'm screaming some more and even wailing, at one point, "Ohhh, Momma." The gun is pointed at my stomach. I put my hand on it and push it away, thinking, "now I will find out what it's like to be shot," and wait for the blaze and the impact. Seconds go by; it keeps not happening. There's a low brick building on the corner with high windows and a chest-high hedge along the wall. He's pushing me toward a white station wagon parked about four cars in from the corner. I veer toward the hedge and bargain, absurdly:

"How about the bushes? Anywhere but the car."

"No," a grunt as he drags me off the curb to the driver's side of the car, opens the door and shoves me in. I grab onto the steering wheel and resist moving to the passenger side. He throws the gun on the seat beside me, somehow gets one arm around behind me, and presses the knife— a bayonet—into the black fur coat covering my stomach.

"Now you're dead," he snarls.

"No I'm not!"

I push at the knife with the palm of my hand, twisting and fighting to get out of the car.

"Hey! What're you doing?" A man shouts from the front step of the office building. Another hovers in the doorway, straining to see what's going on. Tyrannosaurus rex lets go of me and stands by the car door as if he's confused, can't think what to do for a moment. I jump out and run and crouch behind the cars in back of him. In a bizarre, polite charade, he shouts to the men, "Do you want me?"

"No, we don't want you!"

"Get his license number, get his license number," I scream as he jumps into the car and drives off. They take me inside to call the police. My coat has a one-inch slit near the mid-section; the base of my hand is bleeding from a small incision.

For a few days after the attack the muscles in my abdomen hurt. I had never screamed like that. It was hard to sleep in my one-room apartment, with its door on the alley. The door had a full-length glass panel covered with white rice paper, and at night I lay in my bed with my feet toward the door imagining a man kicking it in with the force of an explosion.

I felt triumphant to have escaped; and at the same time I felt ashamed to feel triumphant. I felt it was bad to gloat, even bad to win. I only allowed myself to feel proud that I had passed an essential test. In a life or death situation, I had perceived danger and had been able to act. The policewoman who interviewed me scolded me for screaming and said that could have made the man more agitated and put me in greater danger of being shot. "You were lucky," she said. I didn't believe it was luck. I knew I had made the right choice.

A couple of weeks later, I was called downtown to see a lineup. Four other women were there; they, too, had escaped from attacks in the University District. We watched, safe behind one-way glass, as the first man walked out into the harsh light and faced us. I felt nothing—just silence, suspense. It was the same with the next man and the next. The fourth man walked into the light and turned. Heat and ice ran through me, not as a thought, but as a return of my body's knowing when I last looked into that face, thick, square, and white.

We all identified him. A week after that, as I headed once again for the bus in a dripping gray Seattle dusk, the face appeared again—staring out of every *Seattle Times* newspaper box. He had confessed to the murders of five missing coeds, and had led the police to their bodies, buried under wet leaves and cold dirt outside the town of North Bend.

Some weeks after the lineup and his confession, there was a hearing of some sort and I sat in a courtroom, looked at this man once again, nodded, and said, yes, that's him. Afterwards, I felt vulnerable. Living in Seattle wasn't the same. I felt afraid if I was alone in a house at night and would put chairs or dressers against the door so that I could sleep.

After the FCC's intervention, KRAB's Board of Directors decided they had to act decisively, take control of the station, show that they could run it responsively. The revolutionary stuff was getting out of hand. A member of the board, and also supposedly my friend, one of the station's founders, took over. He became the station manager. But, out of sympathy for Chuck, he said, he gave Chuck my job. Also, he thought he'd be more comfortable working with Chuck.

Nothing I said or did, nothing about me or my character, my competence, or my emotions, had the slightest effect on the Board or the new station manager. It was as if I didn't exist. The fact that I had been doing a good job and that I wanted to continue doing it had the weight of a gnat.

The station manager, a tall, broad-faced man, withdrew behind an ironic smile. "You can be half-time music director," he said. "that's the only other paid position we have."

The irony and the insult took my breath away. I felt that the fact that Chuck was a man and I wasn't had something to do with the choice, but the Board of Directors seemed an immovable force. There was no one to appeal to.

I took a job waitressing at a Mexican restaurant.

My therapist at the time was Fritz Schmidl, a kindly old man from Vienna, not a psychoanalyst but an analytically trained MSW. One day he put his hands on his desk and leaned toward me. "You know, Margaret," he said, "I never say this to my patients—but you are in such a crazy situation. Your work, your friends, this homicidal maniac—you are in a setting that could ruin a person! I never say this, but my advice to you is—leave town! Go some place normal and get a new start."

That was our last appointment before he went on vacation to Hawaii. He had a heart attack in the hotel swimming pool and died. Shortly after that, I did pack up and leave Seattle, first staying with relatives near Palo Alto, then driving cross country to Aspen for the summer, Boulder for the winter, and finally to meet Lord Sean and Lady Samantha at the World Affairs Conference.

On that afternoon in the high, clear air of Taos, it seemed a little less disturbing to stay and learn more of the Family than to get on a bus and go back to Boulder or Seattle. There was kindness and warmth in some of the faces I was starting to know: Noah, Isabel, Maya. Maybe even Byron. I would stay another day or so and follow the flow.

Perseverance furthers

5

Nine at the beginning means:
Firm seclusion within the family.
Remorse disappears.

The family must form a well-defined unit within which each member
knows his place.

—*I Ching*, Chapter 37. *Chia Jen*/The Family

Ten of us piled into the white van, sitting on the floor or on boxes or on each other, and it racketed along the dirt road out to the highway toward Taos. Thomas was driving; I squeezed in on the floor between Daniel and Samantha. She was going into town to the Gallery House, another of the Family's locations, to work at the day care center. I was going into town to see the Family's various projects and decide what I wanted to do.

Daniel started belting out "I can't get no satisfaction" with a big grin, looking thoroughly satisfied with himself and the morning. As the van rattled and bucked he balanced, crouching, on his toes, tipped over onto my shoulder and righted himself, laughing. Being crammed in among people my own age, off on an adventure, thrilled me. And Daniel struck me as the most beautiful man I had ever seen. He was slender and lithe, dark-eyed and copper colored. I saw the light in his face. Sometimes it happened that I would look at a person and see/feel a special light. I thought of it as synesthesia (a combination of two senses) or as some kind of intuition I couldn't explain. I was disappointed when Daniel got out at the General Store with several others. Thomas drove on, up the hill of the main drag and left through the plaza.

Although it was mid-April, only a few trees were starting to leaf out. At 7,000 feet, the air of Taos felt thin and pale. The plaza looked somnolent, with its ancient, brown-washed adobe storefronts, an old man almost the same shade sitting on a bench in front of an art gallery, and a few flashy store displays of silver and turquoise jewelry.

Sean, Samantha, and I got out at the Gallery House, a fine old two-story adobe a few blocks off the plaza. The day care center was on the ground floor in a wide, high-ceilinged room that was full of light from divided windows that opened onto the street. Two rooms upstairs housed the Family's creative projects: a darkroom, and next to it the Graphics room. A sign on the Graphics room door said, "We are the losers who decided to become winners." Here Sean and George worked on their latest brainstorm, a magazine they called *Eupsychia*. *Eupsychia* (eu = good, psyche = mind, soul, self) would focus on the theory and practice of psychological healing. It would be revolutionary, Sean said: "It'll blow *Psychology Today* right off the stands." The first issue was almost done.

A loft above the Graphics room held the "movieola," Sean told me. He took me up the narrow stairs to see. It was a flatbed cart with two film reels on metal arms about two feet apart. "We're making a movie about the Taos communes. Lord George used to be a director in Hollywood, and we're all the crew. We edited it here in this room." I was impressed, and stared through the attic gloom at the simple-looking setup. They ran the film by hand through a viewer and then cut and spliced it on a narrow holder between the two reels.

46

"Where's the movie?" I asked. Sean said it was all done, and that Lord George had taken the work print to Los Angeles to get the sound finished and the negative cut. I wondered how a group of misfits and losers could master all that and make a good film. Sean went on to explain that a local nonprofit foundation called Lorien had given the Family a grant of $20,000 to make the film and have it professionally processed, with Moog synthesizer music for the sound track. They called it *Peace, Love, Two Hours: Taos 1970*. George, Byron, and Sean were working up a distribution plan.

"This thing is really going to take off," Sean said, all lit up with the excitement of it, his hair askew and his brown eyes gleaming behind his glasses. He put a hand on my shoulder.

"Too bad it's finished, or you could have worked on it," he said. "But you could write for the magazine, or take pictures for it. It's going to have great graphics."

We clattered down the stairs to look at the darkroom, which had been cobbled together inside a tiny bathroom. It had all the equipment familiar to me from the Center of the Eye; the enlarger, the red light, the trays for developer, stop bath, and water bath. I yearned to get to work. The school's director had loaned me a camera, an old Pentax, and let me take courses for free while I worked as her assistant. I had discovered a passion for images and for the unexpectedly dynamic phase of photography when the image slowly comes up in the developer. Especially as a portrait emerged, glowing in the dim light, I could see so much more of the person revealed in the moment. There is magic to a good photograph, an intuitive resting point when the eye and the lens become their most receptive, and the shutter clicks. I rarely reached that magic but treasured it.

"Wow," I said, "you mean I could use this?"

"Sure, nobody else is using it right now. There's plenty of chemicals under the sink."

Some internal rubber band kept pulling me back to graduate school, but each time I dropped out, I gravitated toward the media. I hesitated, however, to go all the way into writing or photography. I didn't think of myself as creative. At the *Los Angeles Free Press* I answered the phones, occasionally helped with pasteup, and wrote only two or three articles over the six months or so I was there. Lord Sean had no such self-restraint, nor did he expect it of me.

"Do anything you want," he said. I looked incredulous. He laughed.

"See? That's what it's about. You can be anything you want to be. There are no mistakes to be made."

He opened a door across from the Graphics room. "This is Byron's office," he said meaningfully, as if I should be impressed. The narrow room had an old desk and chair, a window at one end, and a short table holding a CB radio. There was a cot under the window with a dark-green army blanket across it. "Sometimes he sleeps here. We can always call him on the CB radio at the house."

Sean left me to explore the darkroom. Downstairs, the children were arriving, along with two other women who were helping Samantha. The children's voices drifted up the stairs. I decided to develop and print the roll of film I had in my camera. The darkroom was one place where hours could pass for me like minutes, full of life. When I emerged, the Graphics room was quiet; Sean was hunched over his typewriter. I set out for the plaza to buy more film.

Outside, the world was beige: white-beige dirt, grey-beige pavement, brown-beige adobe walls. Spanish-style houses with their backs turned to the street separated me from the community of those who lived there, had always lived there, and weren't hippies. So much lay beneath the surface. D. H. Lawrence had lived here, and Taos had inspired other artists and writers, but where were they now? Where was the Taos Pueblo? Where and who were the Indians? The magical sky of the Indian painting that had hung in my childhood home curved over this town and these mountains. I hoped to touch that magic somehow.

I bought a couple of rolls of black-and-white film and wandered around looking for light and shadow on doorways, textures of adobe walls, the occasional opportunity for a portrait. The town seemed deserted, except for the shopkeepers. An Anglo woman tending an art gallery on the plaza let me photograph her. Her tanned and finely wrinkled skin suggested about fifty years in the sun, while her grooming and condescension suggested money. Her understated silver and turquoise jewelry set off the tan. The gallery featured large oil portraits and Southwest landscapes, priced between several hundred and several thousand dollars. What a contrast to the meager fields, the dry air, the empty sidewalks!

A young couple in a VW van inching through the plaza stopped beside me, and the girl, sweetfaced and bedecked in an Indian bedspread print, asked if I knew the way to the Hog Farm (a rural commune). I didn't, but hitched a ride with them to the General Store, where they could get their information and I could see the other part of the Family's scene. The General Store was dark and crowded with bulk food barrels, ripe with the smells of grains and fruits. Whiffs of woodsmoke, patchouli, and sweat emanated from a few hip shoppers in a swirl of long, braided hair, homespun fabrics, and earth colors. I saw Daniel, busy behind the counter. He flashed a smile and I felt a happy shiver in response.

The free clinic, called La Clinica, although local Spanish speakers gave it a wide berth, was next door. A sandy-haired man about my age sat on the corner of the desk in the anteroom, chatting with Lady Heather, the receptionist of the day. He wasn't wearing a white coat, but introduced himself as the doctor. I dropped into my graduate student inquiring mode and asked some questions about the clinic. He explained that he was an intern from the University of Oklahoma, "gettin' an idea of what a rural practice is like." He was tall and clean and healthy, like a young man from a good family, but without any trace of arrogance. He said the clinic was started two years before by two local physicians and some leaders of the hip community. The university provided interns on six-month rotations and some funding; the rest came from Lorien.

Charlie eased himself off the desk and stood respectfully as Dr. Rosen walked in. The doctor paused at the threshold, taking in the three of us, and smiled. A slightly florid but compact, fit-looking man, he had been one of the only two general practitioners in this small community for some twenty-five years. He seemed glad to have time to chat, and asked me a little about myself. I asked him how it was to live in such an isolated place. He said he liked it, and that it was a good community. He had raised his family here and his kids were now in college. He and his wife occasionally drove to Albuquerque for plays, concerts, and movies, and that was enough. He read a lot. To me he was a prince from another world, another social stratum than the one I was in. I yearned toward him as if I stood on the outer rim of a moat. His castle was his confidence, his birthright. If only Dr. Rosen would adopt me. . . . Charlie offered me a ride back to the Gallery House.

In the late afternoon Thomas brought the van around and took Samantha, Sean, and me home. The house was quiet; it seemed a good time to read or nap, and I decided to throw the *I Ching,* The Chinese Book of Changes. Perhaps I could find a clue to my future in the ancient oracle.

What should I do? What would prove, in the end, to have been the right choice? Making decisions like this was an agony. I imagined myself getting on the bus, the long ride, stepping out at the bus station in Boulder, walking into the apartment where my roommate would look up from her coffee in welcoming surprise. I imagined a long string of days in Taos, eating, sleeping, and working in the companionship of the Family, perhaps taking photographs for the magazine. Each possible future looked equally real. "It doesn't really matter what I do," I told myself.

This was not the first time I had consulted the *I Ching.* Friends in Boulder had introduced me to the idea of throwing coins or yarrow stalks and asking the oracle a question. I liked it better than the Tarot cards, which had images of violence and death that, I felt, could be used to intimidate or discourage. The *I Ching* seemed more positive.

I skimmed Carl Jung's foreword to the Wilhelm/Baynes edition. The basic text of the *I Ching* is believed to date back at least three thousand years and to contain fundamental principles of Chinese wisdom. Both Confucius and Lao-Tse wrote parts of the text. It is based on a principle Jung called "synchronicity," "a point of view diametrically opposed to that of causality." The idea is that coincidence is meaningful; the fall of the yarrow stalks or coins coincides with the advice the questioner needs at the moment.

It was not merely part of my training as an anthropologist but part of my entire upbringing—in short, part of my personality as shaped by my culture—to believe that coincidence is *not* meaningful and that random events are random. The most we could do, I believed, would be to stay open to possibilities and seize them when they arose. But an anthropologist must suspend disbelief when investigating another culture.

Suspension of disbelief is the basic artifice that makes fieldwork possible. Of course you know that your own culture has instilled its values and beliefs, and that theoretically you, the anthropologist, are as ethnocentric as the people you're studying; but you must set these values and beliefs aside and compose a neutral mind and a calm, neutral, receptive face, or you're not likely to hear anything you don't already know. I had exercised this skill in odd situations and found it good. For example, suspending disbelief could make a bad movie more enjoyable; a dull party more interesting; a stupid argument more convincing; a liar more charming. So I suspended disbelief in synchronicity and read on.

The *I Ching* sees reality not as a fixed state but as movement, as situations constantly in transition. What is full is in the process of changing to become empty, and vice versa. The oracle indicates the direction of change in a given situation and suggests the right type of action to take. If the situation described in the book seems wholly foreign, e.g. "Perchance the army carries corpses in the wagon . . ." one can pore over the interpretive paragraph to figure out how to see it as a metaphor. Otherwise, of course, that line can be ignored. There are many ways to read an oracle.

Sitting on top of the mattresses in the Family living room, I threw three pennies six times and recorded the pattern of heads and tails as a straight line, a broken line, or a changing line. This produced a "hexagram" made up of two "trigrams," each with a name and an associated element: in this case, the trigram *Sun*, associated with "the gentle, or wind," over *Tui*, "the joyous, or lake." This corresponded to Chapter 61, *Chung Fu*/Inner Truth. I read the first two sentences:

> *The wind blows over the lake and stirs the surface of the water. Thus visible effects of the invisible manifest themselves. . . This indicates a heart free of prejudices and therefore open to truth.*

I hoped it was true that my heart was open to truth. So far, however, I saw no hint about what I should do. I moved on:

> *Inner truth. Pigs and fishes.*
> *Good fortune.*
> *It furthers one to cross the great water.*
> *Perseverance furthers.*

To cross the great water? This didn't sound applicable to northern New Mexico. But perhaps "perseverance furthers" meant that I should stay in the Family?

Pigs and fishes are the least intelligent of all animals and therefore the most difficult to influence. . . In dealing with persons as intractable and as difficult to influence as a pig or a fish . . . One must first rid oneself of all prejudice and, so to speak, let the psyche of the other person act on one without restraint. Then one will establish contact with him, understand and gain power over him.

In this case, I wondered who was the pig, who the fish, and who the wise influencer. I read on, past puzzling, archaic advice about criminal cases and the administration of justice. I skipped to the changing line—the message most specially intended for me.

He finds a comrade.
Now he beats the drum, now he stops.
Now he sobs, now he sings.
Here the source of a man's strength lies not in himself but in his relation to other people. No matter how close to them he may be, if his center of gravity depends on them, he is inevitably tossed to and fro between joy and sorrow.

Hmmm. Sounded like the Family. Sounded like me. But was that good or bad? Should I try to change it? I read on:

Here we have only the statement of the law that this is so. Whether this condition is felt to be an affliction or the supreme happiness of love is left to the subjective verdict of the person concerned.

In the meantime I had been vaguely aware that somebody in the Green Room had called a Gestalt to focus on Stanley. I was not paying much attention until I heard April's voice, usually soft, raised to a fishwife pitch.

"You're just so nowhere, Stanley. You haven't got the faintest idea where you're at." He murmured something. "That's just it! It's like you're not even in there! Can you find one single thing that you feel or you want or you even think?"

I put the Ching down, went through the kitchen, and found a space inside the door of the Green Room. Stanley sat in the "Nirvana seat," a straight-backed chair, looking far from enlightened. He nervously picked at himself—a cuticle, a zit, his shirttail—and looked at the floor, the bed, or somebody's feet, anywhere but straight into those accusing eyes.

"I'm not a very confident person," he said. April gave Isabel a knowing look.

"No shit."

"What's the thing you feel the least confident about?" Daniel inquired, not unkindly. Stanley pondered.

"I guess it's my, uh, my body."

"Your body? You mean how it looks or what?"

"Well, yeah, I mean I'm not very strong or anything but I guess the main thing is, well, it's my dick."

"Your dick? You mean your penis?"

"Yeah, my penis." Stanley, with his baby flesh, flaky skin, dandruff hair, pallid eyes, and blank expression, was worried about whether his penis was too small. He felt ashamed, he finally said.

"Huh," Daniel grunted. "Too small for what? Can you piss okay?" There were some chuckles at that and Stanley managed a wan smile.

Lord Sean stepped in. "Most adolescents feel some anxiety about the development of their genitals," he said, as if to a class of undergraduates. "Probably the best thing you could do is go public with it." Stanley blinked and stared.

"Go public?"

"Yeah. The best way to get over being ashamed is to get it out in the open and get okay with it. Take off your pants."

"My pants?" Stanley echoed.

"Sure. Go around naked for a while. See how that feels. It can't be any worse than you feel already. Give it a try." Poor Stanley. I decided to go back to the *I Ching*. An hour or so later I went outside and there he was, wandering around looking almost happy in a doubtful way, wearing only a faded blue and grey shirt. His penis, too short to hang, formed a pocket of flesh between his legs, but there it was, and he actually did look more fully present than I had ever seen him.

I went over to him and congratulated him. "My breasts are too small," I said. "I should walk around with my top half naked." I had no intention of taking my blouse off. But an impulse arose to make an even more generous gesture. I leaned over and kissed his little appendage. It felt dry and cold on my lips, mildly disgusting, but I straightened up and smiled at him. He smiled back. Byron was walking by. He stopped in his tracks.

"Far out," he said approvingly, and moved on. Perhaps to him we were the pigs and fishes.

That night after dinner, a group of ten or so were sitting around in the Green Room. Lady April looked at me appraisingly. "Let's find her a new name," she said. My throat constricted. I had always thought Margaret sounded prissy and uptight, but it was my name. They might come up with something worse, or something like "Rainbow" that would be too embarrassing to use. Laura, Isabel, and Heather, who were sprawled out on the bed, sat up and gathered around. They obviously loved this idea. I perched awkwardly on the edge of the bed next to April, who, with her long chestnut hair, wide pregnant belly, and motherly air, awed me. William and Stanley sat on the floor at our feet. Out of a thoughtful silence, Heather said, "I think—Lily." A chorus of yesses.

"Do you like it?" April asked. I did.

Later, as I crossed the Green Room on my way to bed on the living room floor, Daniel was sitting on his bed, leaning against the wall with one leg tucked up, contemplatively chewing a twig. In loose white cotton pants and shirt, with his short-cropped black hair and copper skin, he looked like Toshiro Mifune, one of my movie idols. In *Yojimbo* and other classic Samurai movies, Mifune played the man I would always want on my side, handsome and strong, but above all, kind. Self-contained and yet fully attentive to the human condition, he was invincible in battle, but he rarely and reluctantly killed. My heart thumped as Daniel said "Good night, Lily," with a teasing grin, twig bobbing against white teeth and smooth lips.

Penetrating clarity of judgment

6

In nature, it is the wind that disperses the gathered clouds, leaving the sky clear and serene. In human life it is penetrating clarity of judgment that thwarts all dark hidden motives.

—*I Ching*, Chapter 57. *Sun*/The Gentle (The Penetrating, Wind)

On the way into town the next morning, the van stopped to pick up a hitchhiker, a longhaired, bearded man in a fringed leather jacket. He climbed in and sat down on the bundle he had been carrying, an army surplus sleeping bag stuffed with clothes. With a companionable smile all around, he said he was moving into town because of the violence at the hot springs. Daniel nodded, keeping his eyes narrowed and avoiding looking directly into the hitchhiker's eyes.

"Kind of a hassle, but oh well," the hitchhiker said to Samantha, who murmured sympathetically and then became engrossed in staring at the highway ahead. I wondered why they were ignoring him. After the man got out at the head shop on the outskirts of town, I asked if they knew him.

"No, I've never seen him before," Daniel said. "But with a vibe like that, I don't want to."

"Vibe? What vibe?" I said. "I thought he was just being friendly."

Heather, sitting up front with Thomas, had turned around and leaned through the gap between the seats to admonish me. "You think too much. If you were in your feelings you would've known. That guy was so uptight he was a fight waiting to happen."

"Huh. You sure saw something different than I saw."

"Well, maybe if you get more in touch with yourself you'll start to see more." Although her tone made this a putdown, I took it meekly. I believed her.

We had reached the General Store and Heather, Daniel, and James Joseph got out and headed for work at the cash register and the Information Center. I now imagined the IC as a triage station, where the good apples were directed toward food, shelter, and whatever else their good vibes had earned them, while the bad apples got vague pleasantries and a suggestion to go somewhere else.

At the time, I had not been to the hot springs near town, and had only the vaguest perception that there was some trouble regarding the hippies. Later, on a visit to Taos in 2002, I gathered some background and visited the place, now peaceful, a small eye of blue water at the base of a hillside. A longtime Taos resident explained that the site was sacred to the Taos Indians. Now the Taos Pueblo owns it, but in the past, it was on private land. By tacit permission, anyone local enough to know how to get there could use it. Taoseños and other native people went there for yearly ceremonies; others came to it for healing and meditation, and still others for late-night parties. For many years, all these uses had gone on peacefully.

In 1968, however, the land across the ravine had been sold to Anglos. Two or three houses went up—intuitive structures with earthen or pebble floors, passive solar heating, unvarnished wooden beams and posts, and rounded openings to catch the high desert light. Several families formed a commune named Five Star. A group of bikers also frequented the spring, getting along reasonably well with the commune people, at least on the level of sharing dope and beer. But these groups also overlapped with young local Hispanic men, who were getting angry about the sheer numbers and style of the hippie invasion. Gunshots were heard occasionally around this once-quiet spot; there were fights, and people were getting hurt.

In early April 1970, someone burned down a house at Five Star and beat up some of the longhairs living there. Soon after I arrived in the Family, I heard that "Chicanos" had fired a few shots through the windows of the General Store. (Members of the Family called local Spanish speakers Chicanos, apparently in ignorance of the fact that most Northern New Mexicans of that time called themselves Spanish-Americans.)

Byron and several of the other men—Noah, Daniel, James Joseph, and Thomas—went into a huddle and worked themselves up over the threat to the Family's security. They decided to organize all the men into patrols to guard the house and the General Store. The women kept a fairly normal routine, going into town for work during the day and staying at home with the babies at night, but the men drove around in pairs all night, keeping in touch by CB radio with each other and Byron. The CB radio in the kitchen took on a new and spectacularly noisy life.

"This is Thomas. Come in, Control." (Byron, in his office at the Gallery House, was "Control.")

"This is Control. Where are you, Thomas?"

"Corner of Ranchitos and Ledoux. Looks quiet. Request instructions."

"Proceed down Ranchitos."

"Ten-four."

There was lots of suspense, but nothing much was happening. It felt like a John Wayne movie with a hippie costume designer. As the patrol wore on into a week, the men got touchy from lack of sleep. Thomas, usually cheerful, became morose. He drank coffee to compensate, and his hands shook. The women worried over him, urging him to eat and sleep, but Byron gave him day and night responsibilities, saying that Thomas was the most sensible and we needed him around in case things got out of hand.

The second night of the patrol, Daniel came to the house around 10 or 11 p.m. and said Byron would like to see me. He spoke respectfully, as if I were being invited to an audience with the king. I said okay, but wondered what I was getting into. Because of the respect others had for him, I felt flattered and curious. I knew every woman in the Family was expected to sleep with Byron, but I had seen very little of him since meeting him on the first day. He had seemed humorous and gentle then. He slept at the Gallery House in town, worked at the General Store during the day, and visited the house in Llano Quemado only rarely, with some purpose that didn't involve me. Once the patrol started, Byron was entirely occupied with the men's business, and I thought that was kind of silly—boys playing war.

William and Don, both relative newcomers, like me, drove me to town in the Mustang, speaking very little and maintaining an air of hushed importance. They escorted me from the car to the porch of the Gallery House. I saw Byron holding the door halfway open with one hand, his face visible in the dim light and his brown body blending into the darkness of the interior. My breath caught as I realized he was naked. I could see his bare chest, thighs, knees, bare feet; his rounded belly hid his sex. He smiled like a gracious host and gestured me in. They asked him if that was all. He nodded, and they turned back to the car. He closed the door. I felt a flash of fear. Trapped. Not an audience but an initiation.

"Thanks for coming," Byron said. "Don't worry, you don't have to do anything you don't want to do."

He put his hand on my waist and guided me up the stairs toward the dim light coming from his office, where he slept. The light came from the lamp on his desk. The CB radio sat on a shelf above it. Byron switched it off.

"They'll do okay without me for a while," he said with a chuckle. "I've been wanting to get to know you better. I'm sorry it's taken so long."

"That's okay," I murmured. My legs were shaking a little.

"Would you like some coffee or some water? I'll get you something from the kitchen," he said.

"Sure, some water." He went back out the door and I heard his soft footsteps going down the stairs. There was nowhere to sit but the desk chair or the bed. I took the chair. When Byron came back, he handed me the water and looked down at me sympathetically.

"I know this must seem a little strange to you."

"Yeah, it does." I smiled. I felt relieved that he acknowledged the strangeness.

"How's it going for you?"

"Mixed, I guess."

He moved behind me, put his hands on my shoulders, pressed into my tight muscles with his thumbs, kneaded and stroked until I responded to the warmth of his hands and his skillful pressure. My shoulders gave in incrementally and soon he was stroking my collarbones and then my breasts. I felt relaxed and excited. The rest was easy.

Afterwards, Byron and I lay back, looking up at the ceiling and talking. Byron said he made love to me because he wanted to, but that he made love to Stephanie because she didn't want to. (In the Family, we always called sex *making love*.)

He said, with a comfortable chuckle, "I tell all the new girls, eventually you will sleep with me."

He said that the secret of lovemaking is that you become the other person's slave.

"Your slightest desire is my command."

He added that the secret of leadership is the same thing; the leader is really the subordinate of his followers because he must understand what they truly want and give it to them. He said, "I figured that out for myself; I could see it. But I studied psychology, too."

"Hunh," I mumbled. This seemed to leave something out. What does the *leader* truly want? I thought of the passage in the *I Ching* about pigs and fishes: in order to influence them, the oracle says, you have to let them impress their nature upon you. But that's only the first step. A truly lasting bond must be based on "what is right."

"I'm not the leader because it's necessarily what I want to be," he said. "It's just that I can do it and it needs to be done. I'm a loner. I'd rather be by myself."

In a way, he was by himself. He had privacy and a place of his own at the Gallery House, unlike any other Family member.

I was almost asleep when Byron asked if I had ever tried to astral-project.

"No, what's that?"

"Close your eyes. Can you change the colors you see with your eyes closed?"

I've never been too good at visualization exercises, but I closed my eyes and tried to change a vague red spot to blue. It sort of worked.

"Good. Now focus the light into one spot of light in front of you."

I couldn't. All I could get was two, one in front of each eye. Byron gave up the effort, fell silent, and relaxed into sleep. I lay awake for a while, my head uncomfortably on his shoulder, one side warm against him and the other cold where the Army blanket didn't quite cover. I woke up in the morning with a crick in my neck.

The next evening, when the men were out on patrol again, Gretchen and I were washing the dinner dishes and I asked her about astral projection. She said she had done it several times, and that she had once met Daniel and Byron somewhere over the Rio Grande and they all went flying around.

I still didn't have a specific assignment, so I hung out at home or the Gallery House and joined in the projects of the moment or the endless conversations about the contents of my head or someone else's. William, although he didn't have a title yet, seemed to understand the Family's way of doing things and liked to explain it to me.

"No one is ever asked to leave," he said. "Anyone willing to live as we do can stay."

"But what about that awful Gestalt session with Stanley the other day?" I asked. "People were really putting him down."

"Yeah, that's the hard part. We'll tell you exactly what we think of you, but it's your decision whether you stay or leave. Some people can't take that much of the truth."

"Is it the truth or is it just somebody else's feelings about you?"

"A lot of people are too fucked up when they first join to know where they're really at. Like me." He put one paw on his chest and bowed his head in a self-deprecating gesture that reminded me of the Cowardly Lion.

It was William who told me that Byron had been in San Quentin for armed robbery.

"He learned a lot from prison," William said. "You have to if you want to survive."

I wondered if Byron had acquired some of his charm there. Charm is manipulative; it's the ability to disarm in a pleasant way, and I could imagine it coming in handy among violent men. Like William, I was willing to believe that I was too fucked up to recognize the truth about myself or anyone else. The fact that Byron had been in prison didn't frighten me; it aroused sympathy and respect. I felt that I had never been tested to the same degree.

One afternoon, Lady Heather decided to instruct me in consulting the *I Ching*. I wasn't very good at making up questions for the book, since I didn't really believe it would give me any answers. I settled into a generalized request for a reading—"Where am I *at* right now?" In the Family, this phrase didn't mean the same as "Where am I?" It referred to psychological space, not geographic location.

Heather watched as I threw the coins six times to obtain six lines (the hexagram). We looked up the hexagram in the back of the book to find the chapter to read: Chapter 12, Standstill (Stagnation).

Stagnation didn't sound too good, but some of this chapter made perfect sense, considering where I was at:

> *Heaven and earth are out of communion and all things are benumbed. What is above has no relation to what is below, and on earth confusion and disorder prevail.*

Heather raised one pale eyebrow and cocked her head. I grinned sheepishly.

"OK, I admit that sounds right on," I said.

"Now you get your advice from the changing lines and the second chapter," she said.

On each throw, if all three coins are the same, that is, all heads or all tails, then the line is changing, because it has reached the most it can be of that quality. After fullness comes the downswing into emptiness and vice versa. The changing lines are reversed to make a second hexagram and indicate the second chapter to read.

I had three changing lines, but they might as well have been gibberish:

> *Inferior people who have risen to power illegitimately do not feel equal to the responsibility they have taken upon themselves. . . . This marks a turn for the better.*
>
> *The time of standstill is nearing the point of change into its opposite. Whoever wishes to restore order must feel himself called to the task and have the necessary authority.*

. . . the superior man does not forget danger in his security, nor ruin when he is well established, nor confusion when his affairs are in order.

"What do you make out of that?" I asked.

"Hmm. I think it's saying you're getting closer to getting it together."

That was the most positive thing Heather had ever said to me, so I went on eagerly to the chapter created by reversing the changing lines. It was 57, The Gentle (The Penetrating, Wind).

The Gentle. Success through what is small. It furthers one to have some-where to go. It furthers one to see the great man.

"I don't get this stuff about 'the great man' and the 'superior man' and the 'inferior man' et cetera," I said.

"Oh, you just have to take that kind of intuitively. Maybe it means the inferior and superior parts of yourself, or sometimes it means some-one you know, or else you just ignore it."

Small strength can achieve its purpose only by subordinating itself to an eminent man who is capable of creating order.

"The eminent man again. This is so sexist," I began, but Heather cut me off.

"Don't you get it?"

"No. Do you?"

"Of course. The eminent man is just some part of you. It's like your focus, or your values or something."

I tossed my hair back, tsked, and folded my arms across my chest. "I hate the idea of being subordinated."

Heather chuckled and stood up, lean and plain but somehow cer-tain of her own wisdom. "Maybe you should let that go," she said.

Idly, I threw the coins again with no particular question in mind.

Chapter 44, Coming to Meet:

The maiden is powerful.
One should not marry such a maiden.

****

There seemed an odd disconnect between our whole generation's resentment of outside authority and the Family's acceptance of Byron's authority, which penetrated the smallest decisions in the house. To my practical questions, such as, How do we pay the rent? How much does it cost to feed all of us? Who does the shopping? the most frequent answers were "Byron knows," or "Byron takes care of that." Two or three salaries from the General Store provided the money, but apparently Byron controlled it.

A controversy arose during the patrol week over sending the Family's oldest child, Janine, who was six, to school. The women had agreed that Janine should go to the Montessori school in town rather than staying with the younger kids at the Gallery House and being homeschooled.

"She should have some kids her own age to be with," Isabel told Byron. He opposed the idea. He said it was unnecessary; Janine was doing fine at home. Isabel, April, and Heather (the "boss ladies") talked some more with Janine's mother, Renee, and decided to take the school fee out of the grocery money.

"That's silly," Byron said, "but since you suggested it, you can go ahead and do it." I wondered what would have happened if Byron had opposed the plan. I think the women would have given in without complaint.

"That's a really bad decision," I argued to William. (I was too scared to argue with Byron, Isabel, or the other, "heavier," members.) "Of course Janine should start her education and have contact with people outside the Family. Taking the money out of the grocery budget seems really stupid. How can you feed fifty people on even less?"

"They worked it out," William said. "They hassled it out and came to a decision. If you wanted to change it you should have been there when they were talking about it.

"The rule is that whoever is involved in an issue at the time gets to decide it," he reminded me. "It's a done deal."

"But why should Byron have the last word?"

"Well, he just knows the most of any of us. He's the strongest one."

And that was that. William had no problem with subordination.

That evening I threw the coins again and drew Chapter 6, Conflict. The changing line said:

In a struggle with an enemy of superior strength, retreat is no disgrace.
Timely withdrawal prevents bad consequences.

At the end of the week, no further violence had occurred in town, and Byron called off the patrols. Thomas slept from 5 p.m. until 8 the next morning and emerged tousled and smiling, back in balance. "Thomas is a Libra," his special love, Melinda, told me. "He never freaks out. He just keeps truckin' no matter what."

Fellowship with men

7 *Nine in the third place means:*
He hides weapons in the thicket;
He climbs the high hill in front of it.
For three years he does not rise up.

Here fellowship has changed about to mistrust. Each man distrusts the
other . . . The longer this goes on, the more alienated one becomes.

—*I Ching,* Chapter 13. *Tung Jen*/Fellowship with Men

Lady Maya was going to stay in town for a while at the Gallery House, and she offered me her bed in the White Room while she was gone. It was the bottom bunk next to the door to the Yellow Room. Suzanne slept above it, usually with Jonathan. On the second or third night, I lay in the bunk looking up at the springs above me and listening to the murmurs and shufflings in the next room. A soft male voice spoke my new name.

"Lily?" In the near dark I could make out the features of Sir Richard. "Could I sleep with you?" he asked.

Richard's build, not fat but barrel-chested, and his dark hair and gentle expression reminded me of Alan Bates, another of my movie romances. Richard seemed young and shy, not at all threatening. "Sure," I said, and scrunched over for him. He smelled like Ivory soap and warm body. We cuddled and fell asleep. In the vague morning light as the household was once again stirring, Richard got up and headed for the bathroom. An eager, upside-down face popped into view from the bunk above.

"Didja do it?" Suzanne asked.

"Well, no," I confessed.

"Oh, that's too bad," she said. "Richard's sweet. There'll be another time."

That evening, Maya reclaimed her bed and I was back in the living room with Stanley, William, and another newcomer.

A letter had arrived from my father, forwarded by my mother, whom I had called and given the Family's mailing address.

April 14, 1970

Dear Punker, I hope you are making out all right, wherever you are. We have changed plans and are going to Mead and Wahoo now, then Au Gres. I'm sending this letter and check to Mommy, because I didn't want it to go bouncing around the country. We have been staying with Alberta and Ed the past couple days—it's very nice on the farm. It has really been wonderful, plunked down in this technically modern but socially old-fashioned farm-and-family environment. I am parked on a residential street. The lawns and trees and incidental landscaping, here in Omaha and about everywhere in Nebraska, are amazing. The countryside is beautiful, with so many small streams plus the larger rivers and creeks.

More later. love, Dad

I gave the check to Isabel for the household budget.

At breakfast that morning, when people were milling around dipping oatmeal from a big pot and pouring themselves coffee, Mistress Laura said she wanted me to meet somebody.

"His name was Bill, but he's Kenneth now. He just got here last night from Berkeley, and he's an intellectual, like you. I think you guys have a lot in common." She led me over to the table where a small, thin man sat, holding Laura's baby in both arms as if it were a briefcase. His face looked almost fleshless, with round, blue eyes set deep in their sockets behind metal-framed glasses. He smiled, stretching his mouth ever so slightly and displaying small, widely spaced teeth. Laura took the baby from him and left us alone.

He asked how long I had been in the Family.

"Only about a week," I said. I told him about meeting Sean and Samantha at the World Affairs Conference.

"Sean's really good at explaining the philosophy behind all this," Kenneth said. "I really respect him for that." I agreed.

"What brought you here?" I asked him.

"Oh, I've known Byron a long time."

"Back in Berkeley?"

"Yeah. It's a little hard to get used to the way people treat him now. Before, he was just a man who had something to say."

At this slight criticism, or at least appraisal, of Byron's role, I began to think of Kenneth as a friend. He asked what I was doing before joining and I told him some of my story. When I mentioned anthropology, he brightened.

"That's interesting. I majored in philosophy, but I took a lot of anthropology at Berkeley."

We chatted on in that vein for a while until I noticed the oatmeal was almost gone and disengaged in favor of eating. Kenneth stayed at the table. I took my bowl outside.

Lady April sat by herself on a bench in the morning sun. I veered toward the bench and she patted it, so I sat down.

"How's it going?" she asked.

"I don't know," I said. "It's fun to be here. I don't know if I should stay or not, though."

"*Should* isn't going to get you very far," she said. "What do you want?"

"I don't know," I repeated.

"You seem really uptight. Who are the people you feel close to?"

"Well, Samantha, I guess, and Noah. I'd like to know Daniel and Richard."

"I've noticed you really diggin' the men." She turned to look into my eyes and grinned. "The *good* men. Maybe that's what you're here for. Maybe you'll find your partner here. Who knows? Maybe it's William."

"William?" William, the big lost soul with the greasy hair. "I don't think so."

She giggled and turned back to the sun.

"Just loosen up and follow the flow," she counseled. "Something will happen."

Later in the day, Kenneth and I talked more. His Irish Catholic mother had raised her eight children mostly alone, he said. He was the oldest, and it was understood that he would become a priest. He had smoked marijuana only once and was afraid to try LSD, but he liked the other kinds of freedom he saw in the Haight—the colorful costumes, public hugs and kisses, spontaneous music and dance, laughing and screaming and crying with no restraint. Those freedoms touched his soul, although he didn't think he would ever engage in them. He met Byron in the Haight, where they both volunteered for an aid station run by the Diggers (a radical counterculture group, somewhat anarchistic, that rejected mainstream organization but believed in building face-to-face community). After that, he decided to drop out of the theological seminary.

"That kind of work in the world seems more real to me, more spiritual, than putting on a robe and becoming a cog in the hierarchy of the church," he said.

"That must've been a hard decision. Did you talk to Byron about it?"

"Not directly," Kenneth said, hunching over and clasping his hands together, "but I respect Byron a lot. I think he knows himself thoroughly, more than most people, certainly more than I do." He stared into the yard, his mouth an O of anxiety, his eyes lasering the dirt. "Maybe I'll find what I'm looking for here."

I took his hand and squeezed it and we looked into each other's eyes.

"I hope you do," I said. "I hope I do, too." His arms jerked out to hug me, and I felt the warmth of his flannel shirt and his bony chest against me.

If William was the Cowardly Lion, Kenneth was the Tin Woodsman. And so was I. The Gestalt sessions, especially those led by

Sean, often focused on loosening up those of us who could not or would not readily reveal our feelings. Kenneth and I both were considered too uptight.

"I hate the Gestalts," Kenneth told me. "I can handle myself all right, but I hate them."

"What do you mean, handle yourself?" I asked.

"Oh, I can get through them successfully." He added, "I mean, without breaking down."

It seemed to me that breaking down was the goal Sean was striving for, if breaking down meant losing your dignity and control. When I was on the Nirvana Seat with a circle of people telling me that I was uptight, out of it, and didn't know what I really felt, I broke down. I cried. I wailed. I agreed. Eventually Sean gave up and the session was over.

After one meeting in which Sean frustrated my every attempt to make sense out of what I saw in the group, Kenneth followed me out to the back porch. I didn't want company. I turned on him.

"What are you doing here?"

"I'm with you," he said, kindly. "You'll have to get used to it."

On another day, I was lying on Samantha's bed, one of the double beds in the Green Room, reading, when Kenneth came by. He sat down and I put down the book. He lay down next to me and we talked lazily about this and that without touching, but with a companionable feeling that lasted into the next night, when he asked to share my bed on the floor. Once again he lay beside me, and we slept, without any sexual advances.

I felt impatient. Why wouldn't he want to have sex with me? I broached the subject, gently, I thought, and said that I felt the relationship had reached the point where we should make love.

"I'm not sure I can," Kenneth said. He told me a long story about a frustrated attempt in San Francisco with a woman he "loved very much." I couldn't figure it out. Although I wasn't physically attracted to him, I assumed that sexual intimacy was inevitable. Furthermore, the power I knew I had was the power of my sex, but it wasn't working on him. He seemed to be deliberately withholding something I wanted, and yet I didn't want it very much, but on the other hand did he like me or not?

One afternoon he sat down next to me on the floor of the Graphics room, where I was sorting photographs. The Graphics room, upstairs in the Gallery House, had big windows on the southwest side, and sunlight was streaming in. I was sitting cross-legged with my skirt pulled up over my knees. I asked him what he was feeling.

"I've been thinking a lot about the seminary," he said, eyes downcast and thin lips stretched taut. "My future is such a big puzzle. Sometimes I don't know what I'm doing here. I don't even know what I want."

I felt a rush of contempt. This weak, hung-up wimp, afraid of life—afraid of me. I wanted to show him how much better I was, how uninhibited and wild and free.

I suddenly grabbed his hand. "Here, this is what you want," I said, and, lifting my skirt, put his fingers into my warm, moist vagina. He gasped and said, "Oooohhh. Oh yes. That's what I want." He withdrew his hand, staring at me.

"Well?" I asked, and giggled. I was amazed at myself. I had felt the impulse as an image, perhaps a naughty voice—"Look! Look what you can do!"—and had flung aside the barrier that normally would come up and stop me from doing it. But it didn't have the effect I expected. Kenneth didn't join me there behind the couch playing doctor; nor did he take up my challenge to him as a grown man. He froze in the sunlight.

"I don't know what to say," he said.

Sean came into the room, glanced at us, and sat down at his typewriter. I picked up a shot of children skipping down a hill. At the top of the hill a mesquite tree with tangled branches was backlit by the sun.

"That's a good one," Kenneth said. I didn't answer. He stood up awkwardly and left the room.

Lady Maya had a special friendship with Kenneth, too. I told her that he seemed cold to me and that it bothered me that he wouldn't have sex.

"How can you go on without resenting him?" I asked her.

"I see so much else in him," she said. "He gives me an understanding I need. I don't mind not making love." She looked at me intently, her dark brown eyes soft, compassionate, wise. I felt like a frog, puffed up with resentment and wounded pride.

Lord Sean noticed a tension between Kenneth and me, and so he called a Gestalt session to focus on our relationship.

"What's going on with you two, Lily?" Sean demanded of me, as if I were the one who should know.

"I don't know what he wants," I said.

"You sound angry about that," Sean said.

"Well, I am angry. I'm confused. I wish he would be more direct."

"Where in your body do you feel that wish?"

"That wish? I don't know where I feel it. I just feel confused."

"Where in your body do you feel confused, then?"

"My throat hurts."

"Let that feeling be there." Sean waited for a while for me to allow the feeling to increase. My throat hurt a lot. I started to cry.

The Gestalt went on like that for a while, like an infinite regress. The message was that somehow I had a problem in being angry with Kenneth. The more Sean worked on me, the worse I felt. Kenneth somehow avoided having a role in the dialogue, sometimes staring sadly at me, sometimes huddled against the wall looking fragile, as if he was about to be shot. But, as he said, he was better than I was at "succeeding" in a Gestalt session. He remained tight and controlled while I cried and blamed myself for not being more accepting, more loving, more whatever I should have been according to others in the group.

The next day, Kenneth sat at the desk in the Graphics Room, tilted back in a creaky old wooden desk chair that swiveled. When I walked in, he frowned, turned aside, and pretended to busy himself with some papers. Daniel stood on the other side of the room sorting through some record albums. He glanced at each of us as if reading the temperature. I walked over to the desk, grabbed the seat of the chair with Kenneth in it and heaved him over backwards in a grand thumping clatter. I think maybe he yelled as he hit the floor, and Daniel shouted "Whoa!" and I laughed, feeling a wild mix of rage, surprise, and satisfaction.

"Geez, Lily!" Kenneth stood up without looking at me, found his glasses and righted the chair. "Do you feel better now?" he asked. My heart was pounding and I felt my face flush.

"No," I said.

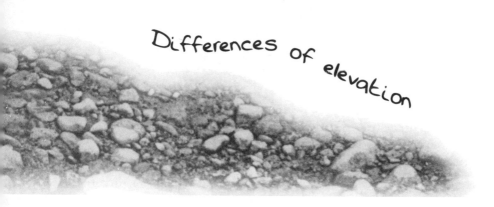

Differences of elevation

8
Heaven above, the lake below:
The image of Treading.
Thus the superior man discriminates between high and low,
And thereby fortifies the thinking of the people.

—*I Ching*, Chapter 10. *Lü*/Treading

Passover began that year the evening of April 20. Somehow it was decided that we would celebrate it. I was not privy to that decision. I was not present whenever and wherever most of the important decisions were made. A member could avoid all group decisions by fading away whenever something "heavy" started; on the other hand, I had the sense that there was an unstated executive committee, starting and ending with Byron, and that a new member like me would simply not recognize the cues, or would not be given the cues, that it was time to talk something over with Byron.

Samantha and Isabel drew up a menu, collected supplies from the General Store, and asked for help at the Gallery House to set up for the Seder. I volunteered. As I hoped, Kenneth did not. We piled bedding into the white van to ferry people into town. The plan was that we would sleep on the floor in the Gallery House and get up early and go to work.

Sir Richard climbed into the van, caught my eye and smiled. Aside from once sharing Maya's bed with him, I didn't know him very well. He worked at the General Store every day, and when he was at home didn't talk much. I imagined he was something like Alan Bates's character in the Ken Russell movie *Women in Love*—kind, intelligent, sensuous.

The main downstairs room where we would sleep held nothing but a battered floor lamp, which filled and softened the space with shadows. The old adobe walls curved up into the whitewashed ceiling, held in place by the long brown arms of the *vigas*. In the shuffle of laying out blankets and cushions, Richard emerged to put his blanket next to mine. He stripped naked and folded his clothes to make a pillow. I did the same, but kept my panties on and shivered a little, although it was not very cold. We pulled up the blankets and cuddled. He mumbled that he was tired from being up all night on patrol, and he wanted to go to sleep.

"Oh yeah, me too," I said. Early in the morning he began stroking me and we finally coupled, trying not to make noise to wake up our neighbors. He came right away and lay on his back to recover. Then he murmured that we would have "plenty of time," got up, picked up his clothes, and left the room. I found that I was still having extraordinary ripples of sensation throughout my body. It felt like an LSD trip with no visual effects, but undulating waves of pleasure. I stood up, hugging myself, folding over and straightening as the waves passed through me, and stepped up on the dais. Maya was standing nearby, wrapped in a white robe and holding her toothbrush.

"I think I'm having an orgasm!" I squeaked. She laughed as if she knew what I meant and was not at all surprised.

"It's the kundalini energy," she said. "Far out, isn't it?"

****

Samantha had risen early to choreograph preparations for the feast. By mid-day an eclectic banquet began to emerge. We would have chicken livers and candied yams, matzoh and turkey and green beans and salad, pie and ice cream and sweet red wine. Five or six women bustled in the kitchen, which connected to the main room behind the dais. Samantha, slender in a white Indian shirt with delicate embroidery, stood calm in the eye of the cooking storm.

A turkey baked in the oven; pots crowded every burner; colanders and measuring cups danced on the counter in a confusion of flour, butter, oil, and herbs. Water ran in the sink. A cloud of steam welled up out of an aluminum pot of boiled potatoes.

Laura and Heather, in heavy restaurant aprons, each took a side of the pot and poured the water off the potatoes. Jennifer trimmed green beans and dropped them into a pan. Leanne, slicing apples absently, stared out the open window to the backyard of packed light earth where her two-year-old daughter, Gina, and two other toddlers played.

"Can I do something?" I asked Leanne.

"Yeah, here, chop some of these walnuts, ok?" I took the knife Leanne offered and arranged some walnuts on a cutting board.

Although Lord George was Gina's father, I never saw him pay any attention to her. Leanne and George joined the commune together, but apparently had split up before that. His main role in the Family had been to direct the film about Taos communes, which was now finished and ready to be distributed.

Leanne had a straightforward, no-bullshit way about her that I liked. She didn't seem to hang around for the Gestalt sessions. She was kind. Although she was thin and flat-chested, even more so than I, she seemed confident. Her bed was in the Green Room, and I noticed that she and Noah often slept together. Perhaps they were special partners.

"I think maybe Byron wants to give a speech tonight," Leanne said, still watching the yard.

"A speech? The same night as Passover?"

"Yeah. George wants to read some scriptures and Byron wants to do his thing, too, so they hassled it out and decided we could do both. It'll be cool."

"Are these all traditional foods?"

"I don't know," Leanne said. "Ask Samantha or George or Sean."

I felt shy about asking questions that would reveal my ignorance. I was raised vaguely Protestant and didn't know anything at all about

Jewish customs, but I had a deep sense of guilt about being of German descent. This despite the fact that my father was at least fifth generation Pennsylvania Dutch (a corruption of Deutsch), and I had never heard him speak a word of German or even refer to being German in any way.

"You were born into guilt," a Seattle astrologer once told me, "and this goes back for many, many lifetimes." Ah, guilt. I certainly acquired it early, if not that early. Although guilt and shame are theoretically separate experiences—guilt an internal punishment and shame a crowd of pointing fingers—there isn't much difference when you're a little kid and you've been caught doing something, or worse yet, feeling something your mother thinks is wrong. "Look what you've done to me!" "You're breaking my heart!" "You're killing me!" The rush of blood to the face—that's the shame—the rapidly beating heart, and then the flood of tears and the wail, "I'm sorry, Mommy . . ." Oh, the guilt.

I'm two or three years old. We're up at the cottage on Saginaw Bay. Momma cooks at the two-burner kerosene stove that perches on green-dotted white oil cloth. The kitchen is a tiny space with a few shelves for dishes and a bench for the stove. The water bucket sits at the end of the bench near the door, the dipper floating with its handle out to one side. I come up the steps into the kitchen and say that I want a cookie. I'm hungry.

Momma says I can't have a cookie before dinner. It'll spoil my appetite.

*But I **want** a cookie, I say.*

No, Momma says.

***I want it I want it I want it!** I escalate into a full-blown tantrum, screaming and stomping my feet. She growls something, wipes her hands on her apron, grabs the dipper and throws cold water in my face. I stop screaming.*

I'm four. My mother stands silently nearby as two people in white gowns with white masks force a metal cone over my face. It smells sweet, sickly, horribly sweet in a way that enters into my nose, my throat, the inside of my head, my lungs, and I struggle to get it off, get it off me, and they hold it down and I know that I will die and they are trying to kill me and I push with all my might, grunting and screaming until I let go and die.

I wake up. I'm in a bed and my stomach hurts. My mother stands by the bed.

"Mommy, I hate you," I say.

She bursts into tears and runs out of the room.

"I'm sorry, I'm sorry . . ." I wail.

I'm eight. It's three p.m. Lunch was half a cheese sandwich and tomato soup at noon. I say that I'm hungry.

"Margaret, you can't be!" my mother says. "You just had lunch!"

I'm twelve. My mother says we're going to go spend the weekend with Helen and Bob. I say I don't want to go.

"Don't be silly," my mother says, "you always have a good time at their house."

"No, I don't," I say. "I don't like them."

"Well, I don't understand how you couldn't like them. I've always liked them," my mother says.

I'm fourteen. I've done something wrong and my mother is yelling at me. I'm angry. She says I look ugly when I'm mad.

"Well, you look like a monkey," I counter. She bursts into tears and runs out of the room.

The list was endless. I knew I'd been bad.

The shame about being German probably came more from family politics than world politics. My mother's side of the family was a mixture of English, Irish, and French, and my mother frequently pointed out that the three unhappy marriages in her large group of siblings, including her own, were all to "Germans" (not German nationals, but, like my father, Americans with German heritage some generations back). According to my mother, Aunt Carolyn dominated Uncle Ray, cooked heavy food, and made him unhappy and fat. Uncle Carl was handsome, but stupid and pigheaded. He had ruined Auntie Mil's life. Howard, my father, was "a dreamer" who never supported her as he should have. She said she only married him because her mother liked him.

As I grew older and learned about Hitler, the Holocaust, and anti-Semitism, it was clear that being either German or anti-Semitic was bad and being Jewish was good. Since I already believed I was bad, I felt guilty and ashamed in relation to Jews, as well as Native Americans, African Americans, and so forth. Those mysterious Others had something that seemed missing or dishonored in my family; when it was present, it broke out, unruly and disheveled, inappropriately loud.

The movie *Never on Sunday* gave me a clearer idea of what might be missing in my own family and culture. When I was fifteen, I saw Melina Mercouri in this tale of a passionate and compassionate Greek woman who happened to be a whore. I had never imagined that a woman could be so open with her anger, her joy, or her sexuality, and still be beautiful, still be loved, and still have the right to say no—never on Sunday—no matter how many men wanted her to say yes. Greeks, Italians, Jews, I envied anyone who seemed to have the freedom to yell and scream, cry and kiss, make up and reach resolution. Expressive cultures—how I wished I had grown up in one.

Now, in the kitchen of this old adobe house in Taos, I would at last get my wish. We were having a Seder and I was part of the "we." Samantha came over and instructed Leanne and me to put the apples and nuts together and add some cinnamon and wine. She said Lord George would explain this dish in the ceremony. Leanne grimaced. "Oh yeah, he loves to explain things."

When the turkey was finally done, we set out the food on a long wooden table, rearranged bouquets of wild flowers and grasses, then lit candles and turned off the overhead lights. Two or three low steps separated this space outside the kitchen from the main room of the Gallery House, and each person filled a plate, then stepped down into the main room and sat on the hardwood floor.

Lord George, full of self-importance and wearing what I thought at the time was a beanie but must have been a yarmulke, stood by the table.

"The first Passover was a time of celebration," he began, raising his voice to an oratorical pitch. He waited for respectful silence, then continued. "God sent ten plagues down on the Egyptians for holding the Jews as slaves, and the last was the worst; he killed every firstborn son. But he told the Jews to mark their doors with the blood of a lamb, and they would be spared."

"Wow, far out," someone murmured.

"They would be passed over. And they were." George looked around for emphasis. "And when the Pharaoh saw that the Jews were spared, and his own people suffered the loss of their firstborn sons, he decided to set the Jews free. But Pharaoh was angry, so he let them go but sent his army after them. They had to run through the desert, and then when they got to the Red Sea, Moses lifted his staff and parted the waters." George picked up a piece of lettuce and the dish of apples and nuts. "We eat these special foods, matzoh and bitter herbs and . . ." Byron, sitting on the top step next to Lady April, interrupted.

"Yeah, George, let's eat. The food's getting cold." George hesitated, and I expected an ugly hassle. I had heard him arguing with Byron once as I passed the door of Byron's office, and they sounded like they would soon come to blows. There was no rule against violence in the Family. But George pursed his lips and lowered his eyes.

"Right, I'll explain more later."

That was the last we heard of Passover.

When everyone had finished eating, Isabel and Heather cleared the food off the table, and others pitched in and moved the table to one side. Samantha and I were in the kitchen scraping and stacking dishes when I felt suddenly overwhelmed with gratitude. The feast reminded me of family gatherings on my mother's side before we moved to California, when most of the aunts, uncles, and cousins still lived in Detroit.

"You know," I said to the sink, "it reminds me of the Chinese saying that if you save a man's life you are responsible for him." Samantha turned to me. As I met her eyes I realized that I had implied that she saved my life by bringing me to the Family.

"I didn't say that," I said.

"Yes you did." She hugged me. I began to cry, and so did she. Then we both laughed and wiped our eyes.

"Come on, you guys." Lady April herded us out of the kitchen and turned off the overhead lights. Most of our fifty or so members sat on the floor in the main room, with the babies and toddlers gathered onto laps so that no one would have to miss Lord Byron's talk. A row of candles illuminated the dais, where Byron stood, his expression an odd combination of humility and command. He wore his usual Levi's, dark leather jacket, and beanie. He raised one hand and the room hushed.

"I want to thank everyone for this beautiful meal and this celebration," he said. "Together we can do everything we ever wanted." He looked around the room and saw wholehearted affirmations. "The Family will take us wherever we want to go. Look at me—all I am *out there* is a black man, a grease monkey, a second-class citizen." He smiled gently and I saw loving faces turned toward him in the candlelight. He went on in a low voice. From my place in the back I strained to hear.

"Some of you know this already. I'm not going to be your leader any more. I'll always be a part of the Family—once in the Family, always in the Family—but I'm not going to be around so much any more."

Daniel, up front near the dais, nodded encouragingly. Byron again gave his curly-mouth smile and looked around. The smile faded into a serious, fatherly expression, and his voice became more resonant.

"Remember that wherever you go, I am with you." Murmurs of assent.

My throat constricted. Did he really say that? And everyone agreed?

"We are becoming the organism of many who act as one."

More yeahs, murmurs. I was holding my breath.

"Pretty soon we won't have to talk like this—we'll have ESP. But for now," he said with a self-deprecating chuckle, "I have another announcement to make."

Byron peered into the crowd. "Kenneth, please come forward." Kenneth stepped up and stood next to Byron, smiling uncertainly.

Byron turned toward him. "I'm a tyrant," he said, "but what the Family needs is a king. Kenneth is the fatherly type. He will be a good king."

I couldn't quite take this in. Why would Byron choose Kenneth, who seemed to hate himself and his own flesh, as a leader?

He took his beanie off and put it on Kenneth's head. "I dub thee King Kenneth." Cheers and applause rose up to the *vigas*. I felt grateful for the darkness.

Kenneth faced the crowd and spoke.

"I didn't ask for this." Although candlelight flickered across his glasses and softened his features, still his tight jaws pulled his mouth into a straight line and he looked erect and thin as an anchorite fresh from his cell. "I don't think I'm qualified, but Byron really wants this and so I'm going to give it a try. But I have a confession to make." Now he was all eyes and twisted mouth, like a Munch portrait of despair. "The king is crazy. The king can't make love."

I gasped but no one else seemed surprised. Why would Kenneth choose this moment to publicly proclaim his weakness or his neurosis or whatever he thought he had?

"We'll help you, man." Daniel, a tall golden shadow, embraced him. Kenneth slumped in Daniel's arms. Others jumped up and crowded around to hug him.

I sat on the hard floor alone.

When Thomas brought the white van around to the front to take people back to the house at Llano Quemado, I climbed in like a sleep-walker and returned to my newcomer's space on the living room floor. I felt close to an essential decision; I would leave. This was just too weird for me.

The next morning Byron told me I would be part of the crew that would take the film on tour. I felt disoriented, spinning.

"But why me?" I asked. "I haven't been here very long."

He patted me kindly and said he was sure I would do a good job. Leanne, Noah, Arthur, and Kenneth would also go, and they would help me. It would be fun. And indeed travel always sounded like fun to me. We would be going to college campuses in the Southwest—places I had never been, but of the sort I knew so well.

Leanne took me to her corner of the Green Room and said she had some better-looking clothes that we should pack for our public show-ings. She pulled out a tailored white dress with buttons down the front, a graceful collar and cuffed sleeves.

"Here, try this on," she said. "I used to wear it when we lived in Hollywood, but I know it'll look good on you." I put it on and she exclaimed that I had class and the dress was perfect for me. Still sleep-walking, I packed some more things for the trip.

That night, I called my mother to tell her I would be travelling for a while. I admitted I wasn't too sure about what I was doing.

"Honey, why don't you just come home?"

"But the film showings will be interesting. We'll be going to univer-sities."

"You're making me sick with worry. Why don't you just take that job in Denver? You could still get it, I'm sure, if you just call the man back."

"Momma, I don't want that job."

"You're wasting your life with this hippie stuff, and you're killing me. It would kill your father if I told him what you're doing."

"I'm sorry."

The receptive brings about sublime success

9

The Receptive brings about sublime success,
Furthering through the perseverance of a mare.
If the superior man undertakes something and tries to lead,
He goes astray;
But if he follows, he finds guidance.

— *I Ching*, Chapter 2. *K'un*/The Receptive

Peace, Love, 2 Hours: Taos 1970, the Family's film, carried a powerful message, according to George and Sean, that would deter other young people from coming to New Mexico. They touted it as a "revolutionary new concept in filmmaking," a documentary made with no script and minimal editing. The crew, made up of commune members trained by Lord George, simply arrived unannounced at several of the local communes and shot whatever was happening that day. They believed that by recording "reality" with no attempt at direction, they could present a truthful picture of the local scene, including the conflicts and violence, the poverty, and the aimlessness of many of the hippies. They also intended it to reveal the dedication and wisdom of some of the communal leaders, especially ours.

"The film is, on the one hand, totally objective," Sean told an enthusiastic audience of mostly Family members at a private showing at the Gallery House, "and on the other totally subjective!"

"It's a whole new synthesis on film," George went on. "The subjective *has become* the objective."

Why was George the director? I asked William.

"Oh, he knows all about it. He directed a film in Hollywood," William reported. "Then he went bankrupt."

On this first showing of the finished film, which had a Moog synthesizer sound track and had been processed professionally in Los Angeles, I couldn't understand most of the dialogue. It was poorly recorded and often took place between speakers with their backs to the camera. Whatever the message was didn't get through to me, although others around me were enjoying it, pointing out people they knew and responding with comments such as "Right on!" and "Far out!" I don't remember much about it except a few vague images of longhairs sitting around outside ramshackle dwellings somewhere in the austere high mesa landscape outside of Taos.

The movie closed with the following exchange, dubbed over a scene of people filing out of a meeting in town:

"What are you dedicated to?"

(Byron's voice, solemn, portentous) "You."

"That's hard to believe."

"I know."

This was considered heavy, an impressive statement of the Family's mission. I had to have William tell me who said what and why it was so important.

Sean and George had been working the phone at the Gallery House to set up film showings on university campuses from Iowa to the West Coast, hoping to build up momentum and pick up a national distributor.

They had scheduled the showings in a sequence from the University of New Mexico, only two hours away in Albuquerque, to the University of Arizona (Tucson), UCLA (Los Angeles), the Pacific Film Archive (Berkeley), and University of Washington (Seattle). They had even managed to find us hosts in most of those places, at least for the nights before and after the showings.

"They're eager out there to meet us," Lord Sean crowed. "They're too scared to change their own lives, but they want to get a taste of it. Smell the sweat."

Late in the afternoon of the day after the Passover ceremony, the five of us left for Albuquerque in the black Mustang. We had two copies of the film and one of the Family credit cards. The name on the card was Arthur Lord. (We all had the same last name.) Behind the wheel, Arthur, pink-cheeked and serious in his dark leather jacket, looked like a boy driving his father's car. Kenneth sat up front in a world of his own. Noah and Leanne and I fit comfortably in back.

The highway out of Ranchos de Taos toward Albuquerque climbs a crest from which the whole valley of Taos and the gorge of the Rio Grande stretch out behind. Far mountains on the western horizon lie dark and unexplored—that way lies Ojo Caliente, the hot springs, and farther still, Abiquiu, Georgia O'Keeffe's home. Looking out the window, I remembered a haunting image of O'Keeffe, photographed by Stieglitz; she looks into his lens with absolute self-presence. It's as if she's looking at herself photographing herself. Where would a woman get that much confidence? I wondered. How did she know herself so well?

Leanne turned and looked out the window across me, as we passed the high rocks and sagebrush that marked the turnoff to Pilar. She said that she and George had stayed at Pilar for a while. I knew that a commune had formed there. They had built three or four houses of organic shapes and local materials, nestled in the canyon on a bend of the Rio Grande.

"It was really disorganized," she said. "They were into drugs, and I didn't want that for Gina." She had a mournful look, even when she smiled. Her eyebrows shaded her eyes and she held her mouth slightly open as if her nose was always a little clogged from crying. Her accent sounded droll to me, but Leanne was always serious.

I asked her how she had found the Family.

"We came to Taos last summer, like everybody else," she said, "and we went to the General Store. Byron was there, and I knew he was going to be important in my life. I knew it when I saw him. He knew it about me, too." While Maya would have delivered this in hushed tones, Leanne simply reported it as a fact.

"George laid a big trip on Byron about being a producer from Hollywood, and he dug it. He could see George was an asshole but he dug it anyway. He invited us to join the Family then, but we had heard about Pilar from somebody in L.A., and George wanted to go there first."

"But why were you with George?" I interrupted.

"I met him at a rock concert in England," she said, wrinkling her nose. "I was young and stupid and impressed. He's very smart, you know. We fucked on a blanket under the stadium. After a couple of days I decided to go off with him, and me mum didn't stop me."

Noah shifted away from her slightly so he could lean his back against the car door and stretch one leg. "Nobody stops you," he said.

Leanne ignored him and went on:

"I didn't want her life. Mum worked all day and then came home and worked some more. George said he'd take me to Hollywood, and he did. We moved in with his parents.

"We had fun at first. George (his name was Edward then) spent his time hustling connections to make his first film. We met a lot of movie people. Some of his father's friends put up some money, and he thought he had a distributor."

"So what happened?" I asked. Leanne shrugged.

"It just went nowhere. He couldn't pay the money back and his parents got uptight." She looked away, toward the split horizon rushing toward us. "I was pregnant then, but he didn't give a shit about that; he just kept trying to get somebody to carry his movie."

"So it wasn't any good?" She started as if I had suddenly switched to Hindustani.

"Who cares? It's all about who you know and who likes you."

Noah nodded. "She's got that right," he affirmed. "There's plenty of bad shit out there and plenty of good shit in the trashcan." Good shit like Noah himself, I thought, and he probably meant that, too. She put her hand on his thigh and continued.

"George is an asshole. Eventually the good vibes gave out, you know? He started hitting me when he felt like it and I finally saw there was no love in him. He's only interested in himself."

"But you stayed with him?"

"Well, yeah, the baby came and I didn't have anywhere else to go. I wasn't going back to England and I didn't have any way to support myself and Gina. I couldn't have gotten any money out of Eddie, so I had to stay with him. We were just *nowhere.*"

Leanne had a way of saying "nowhere" that gave it a lot of force. It reminded me of my favorite Roz Chast cartoon, a drawing of a gray landscape without trees, rocks, or grass, littered with a few pop bottles and torn styrofoam cups. The caption was "Life Without Mozart."

Arthur glanced back at the word "nowhere," then returned his eyes to the road. He slowed down as the road curved and dipped back to the level of the river. Tall cottonwoods, just starting to flesh out pale green, loomed on either side. Grey leaf detritus from last year tattered the asphalt. A small store flashed by; a hand-lettered sign offered "Fresh chiles" from a wooden bin.

"We were together but we weren't sleeping together. He went bankrupt, his parents weren't speaking to us, I thought they were going to kick us out. Then we met this guy at the Griffith Park Love-In . . ."

"No kidding, you were there?" I interrupted again. "That's so far out. I was there, too."

An event that had been a turning point in Leanne's life was a turning point in mine, too. I went there with some of the staff from the *Los Angeles Free Press,* where I was working in the summer of 1967. The *Freep* was one of the first underground newspapers, and I was on my first adventure cycle of dropping out of graduate school. I had not yet taken LSD, and had only recently moved out of my mother's apartment in Tustin to a small duplex in Hollywood a few blocks from the newspaper office.

My roommate, one of the *Freep's* editors, practically dragged me to the Love-In. I didn't know what to expect. What we found was a mummers' pageant, a swirling crowd of colors and costumes. In this huge park of live oak and manzanita, on a hill curving up out of the afternoon smog, a city of strangers became dancers, lovers, children of flowers. Part of the excitement was the deliberate reversal of the way strangers would act in an urban park—no eye contact, each little group in its own social space. In our hugging and even kissing strangers we banished the fear and mistrust that was part of straight society and the world of our parents.

"Be sure to roll up your windows and lock your doors, honey," my father would invariably say when I got into my car. I didn't want to believe the world was that dangerous, and in my experience it usually wasn't. The Griffith Park Love-In was my first emotional, physical experience of The Movement, the first apprehension that there were a lot of us and we were going somewhere.

Leanne and George met a guy at the Love-In who had just come back from Taos and was high with the beauty of the trip, the enchantment of the landscape, and the wide-open communal scene. He told them to go to Pilar.

"But I didn't dig it." Leanne sounded forlorn. She went into town, to Byron, and he renewed the invitation to join his group.

"He took us out to the house and I told Eddie I was staying and I was keeping Gina with me. I didn't care what he wanted. They called a Gestalt and we sat there in the circle screaming at each other until Daniel said, 'So why are you guys staying together?' And that was it. After that, we weren't, even though we were in the same house."

Once the Family had George, they decided to make a movie, with George as director. Somehow his failure in Hollywood had given him more, not less, stature here. For George, the slogan, "We are the losers who decided to become winners," must have had a special cachet. For me it was more ambiguous. I didn't feel like a loser, but on the other hand I had spent my adolescence rejecting the American version of winning, of success. I didn't have any particular image of "winning" that seemed like a good thing. Winning meant competing, triumphing over others, succeeding and, ultimately, finding it hollow as one tasted the hatred or pain of the others. Could that taste be sweet? Maybe to George it was, and that's what we meant by calling him an asshole.

Past Española the traffic thickened, and Leanne became the navigator to find the address of the professor we were going to stay with, close to the University campus. He was a single man in his thirties, I guessed, and an anthropologist. I decided I wouldn't say anything about my own background, but Kenneth told him, almost as soon as we were in the door, that I was an anthropologist too.

"No," I said, "not really, I am . . . I was . . . just a graduate student." But anthropologists always, like members of tribal societies everywhere, must establish their clan identities and search for kinship connections with each other, and so I had to tell him which department I had dropped out of, who my advisors were, and which were my subfields of interest. This was excruciating. I was travelling under a whole new identity, even a new name. If I had met this man at "the meetings"—the annual convention of the American Anthropological Association—I would have tried to impress him with intellectually challenging questions or, better yet, with my *sexy* intellectual questions. Here, I retreated into the group and let the others do the talking for the rest of that evening and most of the next day. That night, Noah, Arthur, and our host played several rounds of chess while Leanne and I watched.

This was the first of many homes or communal groups that opened to us on the film tour. All along the way we found hospitable people, eager to hang out with us, interested in what we were doing and why we were doing it. While at first I wondered why Byron would send me, a new member, out into the world to represent the Family, I soon realized it was a great way to get me to indoctrinate myself. After several nights of explaining our mission and philosophy to audiences, mostly of students and academics, I started believing it. If I hadn't, I would have been hanging even farther out on a limb.

At the time I was aware of the social psychological theory of "cognitive dissonance," but I wasn't thinking about how it applied to me. What it says is that if a group of people believe something that is proven to be false, they are more likely to ignore the proof than to change the belief. The reality of the social situation is more compelling than any other reality. That's why members of cults who predict the end of the world on a specific date don't change their beliefs when the date passes without incident. They still have each other. They simply make up an explanation and move on.

Our first public showing of the film went well. We so impressed the man at the University of New Mexico student center that he forgave the $125 fee for the use of the auditorium and told Leanne, "I don't really understand what you're doing, but keep on doing it."

Later that night, I was sitting out on the back steps listening to distant traffic and watching the moon come up over Sandia Crest, when

Arthur joined me. The Sandia Mountains are a fault block, with a gentle slope on the east side that rises to a pine forest. On the west, facing the city, it's a steep, rocky dropoff with little vegetation but cactus and sage. We turned our faces to the cool wind that seemed to blow from the crest, carrying a hint of pine and dust and sagebrush. He asked me in a kindly way how I was feeling about being on the film tour. I told him I liked it—it was a relief to be out of the house for a while. And how was I feeling about being in the Family? Still unsure of myself, I said, still not sure what I'm doing here and what it's all about.

"Just follow the flow," he said—that Family cliché. "Just stay in your feelings and you'll know. There are no mistakes to be made." We sat a while longer in silence. The moon and the glow of the city blocked out most of the stars.

We left early the next day with Noah driving, Leanne up front, and Kenneth, Arthur and me in the back. I hated sitting next to Kenneth and tried not to let any part of me touch him. He looked out the window, tight-lipped and mute. I looked out the window on the other side, across Arthur.

"Hey, man, you all right back there?" Noah grinned at Arthur in the rearview mirror. Arthur grinned back.

"Yeah, just wake me up when we get there, man." He settled back with his head on his jacket and closed his eyes. I thought of the picture I took the night before of Arthur and Noah looking so wise and intellectual, concentrating on their chess game with the professor looking on.

We stopped for lunch in Flagstaff. Past Flagstaff, the highway drops out of the dry Ponderosa forests and descends the Mogollon rim into the desert. Barrel cacti bloomed red and pink among saguaros, taller than men, like ancestors bearing silent witness. Hot air blasted in through the open windows and we, too, fell silent, each in his own trance.

As I looked out to the east over an undulating plain, the air took on a sudden texture, a flash of brilliance as if the whole landscape was half real, half some other thing. "Stop! Stop!" I blurted out. "Did you see that? Stop, I have to get out." They turned to look at me, dark Noah, pale Kenneth. Arthur woke up. Noah pulled onto the shoulder and I jumped out, staring. It was still there, but I had no idea what it was that I saw. It was just there, like peering into another dimension. I had no words. They didn't see anything that surprised them, but they waited for me and then we went on.

That night in the motel room it was my turn to share a bed with Arthur. It was not particularly my preference or his, it was just the Family's way. We had five people and we paid for three beds. I wore a cotton t-shirt and underpants and he had on beige pajamas speckled with small red cowboy hats. After some settling in I whispered, "What are you thinking?"

"Not much," he whispered back.

"Do you mind if I talk?" I asked.

"No, you can talk. I don't say much because I don't trust what comes out of my mouth." I stared at him, sideways on the pillow.

"What d'you mean?"

"I sound stupid and arrogant most of the time."

"I don't get it," I whispered back. "You seem to know what's going on all the time. You seem really tuned in." He worked on a response.

"Sometimes I hear myself speaking the truth, and I know it's God speaking through me. It surprises me as much as anyone else."

"Huh." I focused on his lips, full and pink, in contrast to the general impression I had of him as an ascetic. He whispered that he could hear other people thinking.

"You *can*? You mean you're psychic?" Immediately I thought what I had always feared I would think if I knew someone could read my thoughts: naughty things. Sex. Penis. Cunt. If he noticed, he wasn't impressed.

"Well, yeah, if you want to call it that. It's no big thing. It's just the same as the other senses—it's just part of the scene."

"Gosh." His skin had a kind of translucence I hadn't noticed before. I had thought of him as rather macho and closed-faced, despite his spirituality, like one of those high school jocks who make fun of anything girlish. Then, too, he never flirted, a fact that made me uncomfortable. I touched his face. His breath smelled sweet. Without thinking, I kissed him and he kissed me back. We made love frantically without speaking, until he came and then lay back in a sweat, like an animal, and said, "I didn't know we were going to do that." This, too, was a surprise—I had assumed we were going to do that. The next day, back on the road, I tried to tell Arthur what I had seen the day before.

"Sometimes I get a special feeling about a place, like a mystical feeling. Does that ever happen to you?"

"No, not really," he said. "Maybe that's your thing. Maybe you have a stronger connection to the earth."

"But you didn't see anything, or see-feel anything, in that place where I wanted to stop?"

"No. But that doesn't mean there wasn't something there. Trust yourself."

We were headed for the University of Arizona for the next showing. George had arranged for us to stay at a place called Oracle, about twenty miles outside of Tucson. These days it's known as the site of the Biosphere, but in 1970, Oracle, Arizona was a mystery, a place you'd only find if someone specifically told you to go there. South of Phoenix we cut over to Highway 79 and drove about a hundred miles through desert scrubland, sometimes rolling, sometimes flat, sometimes with distant mountains on the horizon. When finally it appeared that the road would dead end at the base of a mountain range, we turned left toward Oracle. A few more miles and a dirt road through the mesquite led to a sign, "This Way," and then another sign, "Park Here." Arthur parked the Mustang in the shade of a tree with spreading branches and tiny, feathery leaves like fairy wings.

After the slam of the car doors, there was a grand silence. Above us we could see a two-story adobe house partly obscured by a hill, but our directions sent us up a footpath to the right of it. Something seemed about to happen. Tiny life pulses stirred the bushes as we passed; a lizard skittered away; sun warmth swelled up between sandy embankments as if a Presence were about to speak. We passed one adobe cottage, turned left at a large mesquite with thorny black branches, and ascended another low rise where another adobe stood, freshly whitewashed, with a brown-painted wooden door. A sculpture of found objects—a wacky assemblage of rusting metal and bright bits of plastic in primary colors—suggested this might be a place of laughter. No one was home. The door was unlocked, so we went in to change clothes for our public appearance that night at the University. We left again for Tucson without ever seeing any of the residents, and returned to Oracle in the dark.

I remember the approach; I remember settling down to sleep on the floor of that house, a beautifully worn, old hardwood floor, and I remember our host, Charles Littler, who slept on the floor with us, even though it was his house and he must have had a bed of his own. He was one of the founding members of this place, not exactly a commune but a community of artists who held the land in common but had separate family households. He said there was a central building with a kitchen where they could have community meetings or meals when somebody wanted to, but there was no schedule. Charles had a warmth and kindness about him; he was a professor of art but he was not pretentious, and the whole place had a lightness that impressed me deeply although we were there for only a few hours, most of them asleep. How sensible, I thought, to have a community of separate families and to share this beautiful land. The next morning we left for Los Angeles.

4-25-70

Dear Marion,

. . . Margaret is with a group who have produced a film on Indian life in New Mexico, which they are peddling to various colleges in the West (or near as I can get the message) for adequate fees. The job at Denver General Hospital came through—I told her to try and put it on the back burner and pick up when this movie thing is over. She seems to be healthy and happy but orientation? oy!

. . . love, your brother

Darkening of the light

10 *K'un, earth, above, Li, fire, below. Here the sun has sunk under the earth and is therefore darkened. The name of the hexagram means literally "wounding of the bright."*

—*I Ching*, Chapter 36. *Ming I*/Darkening of the Light

The Anza-Borrego desert floated by, a landscape of old-man Joshua trees and white-shoulder rocks under a clear April sky. Brown smog would filter over the passes later in the year, but there was no trace of it now. In the Family's black Mustang on the way to Los Angeles, I stared out the window in a reverie. Another landscape came to mind, a dry, chaparral-covered slope in southwestern Colorado.

There, a voice blared over the noise of the helicopter: "You must leave this area and return to the viewing stand or you will be in danger of accidental release of radioactivity." I crouched on a rocky hillside, half-under some kind of scratchy shrub, the only thing taller than sagebrush.

My uphill hand, reaching out for balance, landed on sharp pebbles and twigs. I could see David flattening his back against the largest boulder in a jumbled rock pile to my left, and knew his friend John was somewhere on the hill above us. I was breathing hard, partly in excitement, partly from running, partly from fear. As far as we knew, we were on Ground Zero, directly above the shaft containing an atomic bomb that would be detonated two thousand feet below us any minute now. Our assumption was that the authorities would not leave us there during the explosion. Maybe they'd call it off.

David, a man I had met at the *L.A. Free Press*, looked me up in Aspen when I was living there in the summer of 1969. He said an underground nuclear test was scheduled at Rulison, Colorado, about seventy-five miles northwest of Aspen, in dry, rolling hills between Grand Junction and Glenwood Springs. He was working with a Colorado chapter of the Student Peace Union to stage a protest. He wondered if I'd like to join him.

I was profoundly opposed to the use of nuclear weapons, not only for people but also for the earth. The idea of exploding something of incredible force in the bosom of the earth or under the sea—anywhere out of sight—was appalling, as if it would have no effect down there in the dark. The physical adventure of this protest, scrambling under a barbed wire fence and crawling over a hillside, seemed like something I could do.

My courage had failed me two years before at the Century City demonstration against Lyndon Johnson and the Vietnam War. I came away from that feeling ashamed of my own panic. The president arrived at a huge white mall at night in the glare of searchlights. I stood with other protesters, our arms across each other's shoulders, in an outer circle of support for a group, among them my friends from the Freep, who sat on the concrete and refused to disperse. Behind us, LAPD police officers revved their motorcycles and began to charge. I screamed and twisted and blindly flailed at the body of the man next to me. He flashed me a look of surprise and held steady. The cops stopped short of running over our comrades, leapt off and began clubbing them and dragging them away.

Hunting for Ground Zero sounded so much easier. There would be no motorcycles, only the certainty of yielding dirt, sharp branches, shade and sun on the curve of a hill.

The second time the megaphone caught us, the message from the sky was more direct: "Leave this area immediately or you will be forcibly removed." It was dusk. The three of us had worked our way toward the center of the fenced area, trying to stay invisible, but there wasn't much cover. The helicopter hovered directly over us, close enough to blow grit in our eyes and pound us with a terrible noise. John and I dropped to the ground and hunched over, shielding our eyes and ears. David, a tall man with dark hair pushed back in a statesmanlike mane, tried to remain standing, but his hair whipped at his face and he had to throw his arms up to protect his eyes. On the second repetition of the command to leave, David crouched down between us and shouted, "Fuck it, let's go."

Under the helicopter's heavy beat, we crawled back under the fence and walked down the road to a car where two other SPU members waited to pick us up. I felt exhilarated and relieved to sink into the back seat and wipe the grit off my face. We had succeeded, I thought. We had made our statement and we hadn't pushed it to the point of injury, which would have been useless anyway.

I remember no punishment, no confrontation with authorities. We witnessed the test at a small viewing stand with perhaps fifty other people. The bomb went off at 9 p.m., well after dark, so there was nothing to "view"—but something to feel. I sat on the ground with my legs extended toward the distant hill and felt the earth move in a shock wave under me, exactly like an earthquake. Earthquakes were a pleasure of my childhood in Southern California. I grew accustomed to small quakes and relished that sense of the aliveness of the earth. Here, the physical sensation was the same, but the pleasure perverted by the knowledge that this undulation of the earth's crust represented my government's test of its capacity to kill. We three walked back to our car and left without talking, under a spell.

Later that week, David invited me to another new experience; he had some mescaline and was willing to share it at his current home, a campground at 9,000 feet, some ten or twenty miles outside of Aspen. I didn't know him very well, and he was not very communicative. He went off to contemplate the rocks in his own way. I sat by the stream. I leaned against a granite boulder in afternoon sunlight among low bushes, white-trunked aspens, and some kind of conifers. I didn't know their names, but felt that I was learning their essence. The voice of the stream expanded until each passageway between pebbles, each runnel and rivulet spoke separately. As

I looked into the sky I felt it resonate. The air had texture; the boundaries fell away. There was only the absolute suchness of the rock, and myself no more than an empty vessel filled by this pulsing, luminous world.

Later that day, when I came down the mountain into town, I realized that I was no longer willing to eat meat or wear synthetic fabrics, which felt unpleasant on my skin. The vegetarianism lasted about six months, the length of my time working at Fred's Steak House in Boulder. (I never had a steak at Fred's.) I still prefer natural fabrics next to my skin.

As the Mustang approached Cajon Pass, familiar to me since childhood, I came back to the real space of the car and my four companions. We crossed over the pass between rocky hills still faintly green from the rains of February and March. Bright orange California poppies and subtle blue lupines grew in fingers along the slopes. As we entered the smog, visible from the pass as a layer of brown sludge over the Los Angeles basin, the sky above us lost its blue, until it was a thin mucousy grey with a bluish hole at the top.

Kenneth was in a talkative mood and made conversation about the showing at UCLA, who we would stay with, and how much he hated big cities now that he had seen another way of life. Leanne talked about her brother-in-law, Hal, who would put us up for three days.

"I'm really close with him and his wife," she shouted to Kenneth over the noise of our car and the other cars rushing along beside us.

Kenneth turned around in his seat and asked me if I liked being back where I had grown up.

"No," I said, hoping to prevent further questions. "It's weird." I looked out the window at the pink and white oleanders flashing by on the median. Black stripes of tar drawing squares on the road's surface made a whump, whump, whump under the car. I remembered countless trips on this road, hearing this sound, when the freeway was only four lanes instead of eight. After the divorce, my father lived in Los Angeles and would come to Redlands or La Jolla once a month to pick me up for a visit. Later, when I was in high school, I would take the train. After he remarried, he and my stepmother, Elvera, would drive the red camper truck, which he affectionately and not too imaginatively called Blazer (it was a Chevy Blazer), and pick me up for camping trips in the desert beyond Palm Springs or the Sierras beyond Bakersfield. He would always greet my mother with a big kiss on the mouth as Elvera sat in the truck.

My mother always said "El-Veer-ra" with a sardonic twist. She had pursued the divorce, yet she seemed to think of Elvera, a much homelier woman, as a hated rival.

My father and Elvera now lived in Yucaipa, a small community in the foothills of the San Bernardino mountains, but I had not let them know I was travelling near them. My mother lived in Palm Springs, and I hadn't told her, either.

In the smog on the freeway I thought of the clean scent of Elvera's house and the comfort of the hideabed in their spare bedroom. I had written many poems in that room, sitting up on that bed, and I knew intimately the natural places surrounding the house; the dry eucalyptus trees on the blank side wall, the tidy white gravel in front, the dense lawn in back that grew to the cliff-edge of "the wash," a wide ravine that carried water only once or twice a year in a flash flood. Beyond the wash the foothills rolled up into the mountains and on clear days you could see San Gorgonio peak.

It was indeed weird to be so close to my parents without their knowledge. I had talked to my mother by phone twice since joining the Family and had received several letters from her. She worked as a medical transcriptionist and would dash off letters on her typewriter at work. Her last letter, which arrived just before we left Taos, was still tucked into my purse.

My darling daughter—

This typewriter is still cold from sitting overnight so I miss a letter now and then—

However, want to drop you a word or two to let you know I adore you. Remember the kook who came over for champagne when you were here for Christmas? He thinks he is some psychologist (among other things) and reported to Betty that you obviously "hate your mother's guts." I don't know what brought that on but I refuse to accept it cause I know damn well you don't hate my guts, even though there may be times when you don't especially admire me—for which I cannot blame you, since there are times when I don't think much of me either! Anyhow, I love you and love is simply a state of mind in which one loves one's beloved despite small flaws. Therefore, I am sure my daughter loves her stupid old mother—flaws and all. So there.

*Remember how we like black bread? Well, I bought a small loaf
(party loaf) black bread the other day and that's what I had for breakfast
this morning—toasted in the broiler. Yummy, yummy. Got to thinking
about you—hence this.*

*We have been having such beautiful weather here that I detest coming
to work mornings. However, once I get here I get so busy I don't know
whether it is raining or sunny outside until after dark. Wish I could stay
outside and get a good glowing tan.*

*Gotta get to work. The boss is in Phoenix but I'm loaded with work
to do, as usual. Looks like I'll be going to Phoenix about May, unless he
and I have another set-to. In which case, I will probably take off for parts
unknown. Trying to go along with him, though, since I feel this company
offers a pretty good future for me. We shall see.*

I love you. Take care of you and write to me.

Your ever lovin' Mommy

The part about how "we" like black bread irritated me. I don't like
black bread. I've never liked black bread.

The traffic thickened, and the freeways coalesced and twined among
one another like vines falling away from a trellis. We found our exit and
searched through sunny neighborhood streets for George's brother Hal's
house, which turned out to be an elegant, Southern California–style split-
level with a patio and pool. We would stay there three nights and show
the film at UCLA.

Hal was a stockbroker. He seemed kind, reliable, successful, even
dull, in contrast to George. I was impressed that such a "straight" person
would host us. Leanne and Noah babysat Hal and Debbie's two-year-old
boy the first night we were there, and Leanne called home to Taos twice
a day to talk to her own two year old, whom she missed horribly.

In everything we did, whether it was hanging out at Hal's, or going
to the university to make last-minute arrangements, or walking around
in Westwood, or riding in the car, I avoided Kenneth. But the others got
on my case.

"You should work that out," Leanne said. "When you hate someone, they're just your mirror. Whatever it is that you hate in him, it's
something you don't like in yourself."

Noah agreed with her and called a Gestalt session among the five of us in Hal and Debbie's Danish modern living room. I was on the hot seat, a white Naugahyde recliner, with Arthur on one side in a straight-backed chair and Kenneth on the other side, incongruously upright in a black beanbag chair. Leanne and Noah sat like parents on the couch facing me and Kenneth. Purple bougainvillea peered through the picture window behind them, and beyond it lay a Southern California panorama of white stucco houses, lush landscaping, and the deserted, sunlit street.

"Kenneth is just down on himself and up in his head," Noah started out, "Same as you, Lily."

I thought of Noah as my friend, kind and honest, with an easy humanity I yearned for. Here he was, criticizing me. I had been accused of being too much in my head so many times, in encounter groups, in therapy groups, and in the Family. I felt squeezed together inside myself. How could I get out of my head? I began to cry.

Arthur put his hands in his jacket pockets and rocked back in his chair. Kenneth looked uncomfortable.

"I know I should be more open and accepting," I said, sucking in air and stifling my sobs.

Kenneth asked what he could do to help me.

"I don't want you to do anything," I said, not looking at him and still crying in small, jerky bleats.

"Well, Kenneth, what do you want from Lily?" Noah asked. I thought I knew the answer—of course he wanted sex with me, and in some twisted way he must be in love with me, but he was too hung up to do anything about it. His "oooh, yes, that's what I want" replayed in my ears, and the humiliation of his backing away.

"I want her friendship, that's all," Kenneth said. He clicked his eyes on mine for a second, then looked down. My face flushed. The hell he did.

"You want more than that, and I can't give it to you."

No one said anything for a while. I sniffled. Noah leaned forward, resting his hands loosely on his thighs, and looked intently from Kenneth to me.

"I believe you two just got to work it out," Noah said. "Take your time."

"I'm certainly willing to do that," Kenneth said, his arms folded tightly across his chest.

Arthur exhaled. The front legs of his chair clunked on the floor. Leanne said it was time to get the film and head out for the showing.

At UCLA, as at the first two stops, our posters drew a good-sized crowd, but the film itself didn't stir up much excitement. We took turns answering tepid questions. Here there were film students who asked about our equipment. George and the crew had some problems getting the sound in synch. They had used a rented Bolex, a classic camera for documentaries in out-of-the-way places, and a reel-to-reel tape recorder with a microphone that picked up too much background noise.

"Too bad you didn't have a shotgun mike," one of the students said.

"Yeah, man," Arthur grinned at him. "Too bad we didn't have a lot of things. But we learned a lot."

A young man with long hair and love beads over a hip-length tie-dyed shirt wanted to know why we hadn't interviewed more of the leaders—Wavy Gravy of the Hog Farm, Ram Dass of Lama, and whoever owned the land at Morningstar.

"That wasn't our trip," Noah told him. "We had this other idea, that it would be better to just show up each day and shoot whatever was happening. So that way it would be real, and it wouldn't be what anybody had decided the public should know, it would be what was really happening in the commune."

"You didn't have a script?" asked another film student.

"No, nothing."

"That kind of shows," the student went on. "It's real enough, but it's kind of formless."

"That's what we wanted," Leanne said. "Life is formless. There's a lot of hanging out and aimlessness around the communes, and we wanted to show that."

The audience fell silent. The woman sociology professor who had organized this thanked us, the audience clapped dutifully, and the California premiere was over.

That night Leanne and Noah wanted to sleep together, Arthur wanted to sleep alone, and that left one bed for me and Kenneth.

I was furiously opposed to sleeping with him. Nevertheless, the others insisted it would do us good. Besides, they said, there was only the one bed.

I don't remember what the room looked like or what he looked like or what either of us wore to bed. I don't remember what he said or what I said or whether we even said anything. What I do remember is that he wanted sex with me and I didn't want him to touch me.

He threw an arm across me and pulled me to him. I struggled against him but he pinned me down with more weight and strength than I thought he had. Straining and grunting, I hissed through clenched teeth, "Get off of me, you son of a bitch." I expected him to let go. He bore down on top of me, and with my whole body I tried to get him off, to flail at him. He managed to push his penis inside me. He penetrated me ever so slightly, so that I hardly realized he had done it until he gasped and came and let go of me and I rolled away from him and slid onto the floor. The door was open to the other room where Arthur, Noah, and Leanne slept, but all was silent. A clock hummed on the nightstand. I heard Kenneth's heavy breathing gradually subside. I grabbed the bedspread and pulled the whole thing off and wrapped up in it, heart pounding and head thumping with angry, tangled thoughts: Goddamn him. Surprised he could force me. Even Kenneth, who looked so weak, turned out to be stronger than I, simply because he was a man. Sexual dimorphism in primates. Males are, on average, both larger and stronger than females among all the primates, from lemurs to chimpanzees to us. But it didn't hurt. He didn't win. Win what? I still hate him. Eventually I shut down the words, rolled anger into a hard black ball, and fell asleep, hugging myself, wrapped in the bedspread on the floor.

When I woke up the house was still quiet. Despite the thick white rug, my hip and shoulder felt sore. Kenneth lay on the bed with his back to me. I wanted a ritual bath, a circle of old women keening. But when Leanne came into the bathroom as I was finishing my shower, I said nothing. I thought she and the others must have heard us struggling, but I'll never know that. I felt implicated, dirty and guilty. Kenneth didn't look any happier; in fact, if anything, he looked even more tightly wound than usual, but no one asked us anything about our night.

After a noisy breakfast with Debbie and the kids, we repacked the Mustang and left around noon for the next showing, at the Pacific Film Archive in Berkeley. For me it was a numb, silent journey, cooped up once again in the intimacy of the car with four companions that I felt, on that day, I hardly knew. We reached Berkeley around midnight and crashed in a group house. I vaguely remember a green shag rug, sleeping bags on the floor, drab kitchen linoleum and dirty dishes.

Berkeley was the sophisticated city to which my high school friends and I made pilgrimages from our Southern California outback. We idolized the Beatniks, the poets, the philosophers, and the peaceniks, as my father called them. When I was a senior in high school, I traveled with a couple of girlfriends to visit an older brother who studied philosophy at the University of California at Berkeley. He let us stay in his upstairs apartment, which he shared with Willie, a gentle, acne-scarred man always ready for deep conversations about art, politics, or the meaning of life. I had little experience of the Berkeley of the Movement or of San Francisco's Haight Street. I simply thought of Berkeley as a place of very bright people inhabiting the largest possible intellectual world.

That afternoon, the five of us walked up the stone steps of the University Art Museum. Noah carried the film in its metal canister. The director of the Pacific Film Archive had agreed to show *Peace, Love, Two Hours: Taos 1970* to a small, invited group. The director, a well-groomed man in his forties, I guessed, looked smooth all over, polished, calm. He himself was a filmmaker, Lord George had told us, and the creator of the archive. He met us at the door and led us up one flight of stairs to a room where about ten people stood talking, as if at a cocktail party.

The director introduced us as "the communal group who have made a movie about Taos." Among the guests were the poet Gary Snyder and a French woman described as a close associate of Louis Malle. These names meant everything to me; I don't know what they meant to the others. I had seen *Zazie dans le Metro* and Malle's nine-hour documentary, *Phantom India*, and considered him one of the world's great filmmakers. Gary Snyder was, of course, an icon for earth-consciousness and American Buddhism.

While the film was being threaded into the projector, conversation resumed. Kenneth walked over to Gary Snyder and held out his hand.

"It's an honor to meet you. I really love your poems," Kenneth said, looking up at him with unrestrained respect. Next to Snyder, Kenneth looked small and eager, his thin hair combed back from his high, shiny forehead, the delicate bones of his face prominent in the fluorescent light. He didn't look like a man who would rape a woman.

Leanne and I had dressed up for this meeting, she in a slim burgundy skirt and blouse and I in her tailored, long-sleeved white dress. I could feel sweat soaking the rayon under my arms, but I felt cold, too. I realized I was clenching my teeth and made an effort to relax my jaw. I still didn't want to think of it as rape. I thought of it as the night he mounted me, as one chimpanzee mounts another to gain higher status. But what do the chimps on the bottom feel? Do they grind their teeth when they sleep?

The director started the projector. As the rough X-Y markings on the leader flashed on the screen, he doused the lights. I sat down between Leanne and Arthur and the movie began. The now-familiar scenes in the New Mexico landscape expanded; long, unedited minutes rolled by; mumbled dialogue fell into silence; the final scene came on, with hippies filing out of a meeting somewhere and Byron's muffled voiceover, which was intended to convey his selfless dedication to serving others.

The Archive director stopped the projector and set the film to rewind. No one spoke until the celluloid tail flapped and the projector was turned off.

When the lights went up, he gave it to us straight:

"You have some good material here," he said, "but it's too bad you didn't learn your craft."

He told us that the film was poor in nearly every way it could be—poorly conceived, poorly shot, poorly edited—and it had a nearly unintelligible sound track. It wasn't likely to go anywhere.

"I can't give you much support for this," he said. "I'm sorry."

The French woman caught my eye. She pursed her lips and tilted her head slightly in what I interpreted as a look of sympathy.

"It is a start," she said. "Now you can go back and try again. Don't give up."

As the five of us walked down the echoing stairs to the street, I spoke first: "I guess we'd better call George. That was pretty definitive, wasn't it?" No one answered. When we got back to where we were staying, Leanne put in a call to Taos. Soon we had a conference going with George and Sean on the extension. They were unimpressed.

"Aah, they're hung up on content," George said. Sean agreed. "They just don't get it. It's the form that's revolutionary. These guys are just stuck in the past."

"But this is the big world," I said, rubbing my thumb against the rough fingernail of my middle finger. "You couldn't find a much more sophisticated audience."

"Yeah, that's their problem. Sophistication is just another word for uptight mind games," Sean countered.

They had a little festival of criticism, putting down the Berkeley intellectuals and their uptight mind games. Soon Noah, Arthur, Kenneth and Leanne sang the same song. I left the conversation and sat on the arm of a grungy, brown, overstuffed chair. I found the tiny break at the corner of the fingernail and eased it wider with my bottom teeth, then tore off a shred and chewed on it a while. That was the last fingernail long enough to bite. I'd have to wait a few days for the others to grow.

Lakes resting one on the other

11

A lake evaporates upward and thus gradually dries up; but when two lakes are joined they do not dry up so readily, for one replenishes the other.

—*I Ching*, Chapter 58. *Tui*/The Joyous, Lake

A fine mist blurred the lights on the freeway. As the familiar green-signed exits for South Seattle ticked off into the dark, my underlying identity chafed at the new one like itchy skin under a mudpack. Images, faces, feelings I had tried to leave behind by leaving Seattle more than a year ago clamored to be let in. I was sitting up front with Arthur so I could give him directions, and I chattered about Seattle's neighborhoods, the Public Market, the University District, and anything else I could think of to avoid feeling my anxiety.

My friends Mike and Daisy Szabo had offered to put us up at their house. Mike was a young professor of ethnomusicology, Daisy, the

Perfect Woman, his wife. They lived in a slightly rundown two-story house, probably built in the 1920s, with a front porch and old-fashioned split-pane windows. We trailed up the walk breathing in the smell of leaf mold and wood rot, familiar and sweet to me. Mike opened the door, smiling through his droopy mustache (Hungarian with a Latin flair), and hugged me to him. He was soft and round, with startlingly white, freckled skin, black hair, and full lips. He welcomed my companions as if they were visiting dignitaries.

Daisy, elegant and calm, also hugged me and offered her hand to each of the others. Daisy's outward perfection—her air of modesty edged with sharp intelligence, her perfectly balanced features, her grace, her grooming, her shiny blonde hair and golden tanned skin, and her southern-woman appearance of docility when she was with Mike in public, all made her completely incomprehensible to me. Mike loved his own joke: "Daisy's inscrutable—I've been tryin' to scroot her for years."

Although he was rapidly gaining prestige and status in his esoteric field, Mike understood poverty. I was grateful to him for the time he came into the German pastry shop where I was waitressing. His first reaction was, "What are you doing here?" then he said, so respectfully, as if reminding himself, "Oh, of course—working for a living."

Daisy and Mike put us all at ease; soon they had Noah laughing and open, Leanne almost cheerful, Arthur unguarded, even Kenneth looking relaxed. Daisy showed us the spaces available for us to sleep and let us sort ourselves out. I chose the couch on the upstairs sun porch, which had windows looking out into the trees. Leanne and Arthur took the double bed nearby. Noah liked the living room floor and Kenneth took the guest room.

Around ten in the morning when I went downstairs, the house was quiet; Mike was at the University and Daisy had gone to work at an art gallery downtown. A long oak table with batik place mats from Bali took up most of the dining room. Javanese shadow puppets graced the walls in the attitudes typical of their characters—brave Rama, compassionate Sita, and the foolish clown. The round, organic shapes of Japanese pottery contrasted with the red-and-black geometry of the Oaxacan rug. Through the open door to the den I could see Mike's record collection, lining one entire wall, with tapes stacked in boxes and scattered near the phonograph and tape player.

With his knowledge of world music and his generosity in sharing it in any form, this man had changed my life, and most likely those of many others. He had studied the music of the *griots*, the minstrel-storytellers of West Africa, as well as a wide range of Eastern European gypsy music. He spoke several languages fluently. But besides his specializations, he loved all the traditional music of the world. His records and tapes formed the core of the music collection at KRAB-FM, Seattle's "alternative" radio station. At that time, except on KRAB, none of that music could be heard outside of scholarly circles. Mike occasionally recorded programs for KRAB of world music interspersed with poetry or voice-over translations of the lyrics. He and Daisy would read on the air together, their soft voices brushing prose into poetry.

Discovering ethnomusicology was one of the peak experiences of my life. Mine was not a musical family, but from early childhood, the good music that came my way affected me deeply, in a hodgepodge of coincidental ways. When I was four and we moved to Wellington, Ohio, the previous renters had left behind two records: Ferde Grofe's *Grand Canyon Suite* and *Cocktails for Two* by Spike Jones. I adored both and made my parents play them over and over on an old phonograph built into a radio cabinet.

In college my knowledge of music widened, but I never learned to play an instrument and simply described myself as a passionate listener. It was Mike Szabo who gave me the Holy Grace of Sound: music of the pygmies of the Ituri Forest, who alternately blow a one-note flute and sing in a breathy, childlike cadence like spirits of nature; Atahualpa Yupanqui, the great Argentine guitarist, his songs full of sorrow and compassion for the campesino and the forgotten land; Korean P'ansori, a style of singing from deep in the gut that calls down the spirits and buoys up the soul, like Flamenco *cante hondo* (deep song).

Mike was the pusherman in my world, the one who had the sweetest sounds I'd ever heard. He gave his students and friends priceless tips—"Listen to this, here's a really good Brazilian singer—Nara Leao." Or "Have you heard this?—South Indian nagaswaram." Or "Here's a good shakuhachi record." And on into a musical world of wonders.

Mike and I made out for the first time at the Tibetan New Year's party. It was early in my graduate school career, perhaps 1964–65, the first year I was in Seattle. There were several scholars of Tibet at the

University of Washington, and Seattle became an early center for Tibetan refugees. Burgundy-robed lamas could be seen around the University District. I already had an extremely positive stereotype of Tibetans from a few contacts I had when I was travelling in India and Nepal as an exchange student. I thought of them as jolly, openhearted, and lusty, compared to the more formal and inhibited North Indians. I was excited to be invited, along with other anthropology graduate students, to a Tibetan New Year's party.

The party was in a professor's home, an elegant, turn-of-the-century brick house on Capital Hill, with polished wood floors, Persian carpets, and labyrinthine rooms, hallways, nooks, and walk-in closets. Greek music skirled from deep in the living room, and a mixed crowd of graduate students and professors improvised a Greek dance, dipping and bobbing like apples in a bucket. A world authority on African art pirouetted, waving his handkerchief aloft. No Tibetans in sight. Loud talk from the kitchen filled the hallway. I looked around for a place to put my coat.

Dr. Michael Szabo appeared, pudgy yet handsome in a dark, collarless, designer suit and white silk shirt. "Ooohhh, here, let me take that for you," he murmured, caressing my arm and hand on his way to the coat. In one deft movement he had opened a door, revealing an old-fashioned walk-in closet with soft light from above; ushered me in; closed the door; pinned me softly against some of the hanging coats, and kissed and nuzzled my face, neck, ears, throat, murmuring something like ". . . sweet little bird." Thus began a pleasant flirtation, an on-and-off affair, a sort of friendship.

You have to understand: this was one of the highest-status men in my world. I didn't feel exploited, I felt favored. I believed him when he said I was special. The fact that he said things like that in coat closets, his "secret" office, or on afternoons when his wife was not around didn't bother me as much as feeling left out, unattractive, unappreciated.

He could also withdraw his love very effectively, and put the blame on me. I wrote the following exchange in my journal:

Szabo says, "You don't like me."
"Who says?" I ask his vest.
"You charge a high price for your friendship. I have to be so careful with you."

"Well, you don't like me, either."
"Like you? Baby, I love you. You should smile because I love you."
I do smile. Until at the next corner my throat, mouth, nose are pinching
each other shut and . . .

I didn't finish the sentence. Feeling anger wasn't acceptable. Feeling anger toward someone claiming to love me was even unsayable. Besides, I couldn't figure out why I felt angry. I thought it was my fault that I wasn't compliant enough. The fact that he was married, and that I was only one of several graduate students he seduced, including one of my best friends, bothered me, but not very much. It was like the joke Woody Allen tells at the end of *Annie Hall*, which goes something like this:

My brother thinks he's a chicken.

That's crazy . . . why don't you take him to a psychiatrist?

I can't—I need the eggs.

****

Arthur had been up for a while and sat in meditation in the living room. Noah was coming in from a walk. I found cereal and milk and oranges. Soon Leanne and Kenneth wandered in. We had two days until the film showing, and we decided to go downtown, see the Public Market, hang out.

At the Public Market we got into a disagreement about dinner. I was all for getting a bounty of vegetables, fresh herbs, and fruits, but at the fresh fish counter Noah said he wanted lobster. I thought that was a shocking extravagance and suggested red snapper.

"It's cheap, and you can cook it a lot of different ways," I said, but Noah persisted. Arthur took me aside.

"Noah's never had lobster," Arthur told me. "He grew up in the ghetto. This would be really special for him."

"Wow, of course," I said, feeling ashamed of my ignorance. We compromised with one large lobster for Noah and red snapper for the rest.

That night Mike and Daisy took the salad greens, red and green peppers, radishes, carrots, broccoli, fresh basil, cherry tomatoes, baby red potatoes, garlic, fish, and lobster, and made a feast. We helped set the table with the Balinese placemats and flowers from the market. Daisy lit candles and then brought out the lobster, cooked simply with butter and garlic, and set it in front of Noah. He tucked a napkin under his chin and tilted back in his chair to take it all in. He laughed and glowed bronze in the candlelight, spectacularly handsome with his high cheekbones, sparkling eyes, and neatly trimmed goatee. I remembered how closed he had looked to me when I first met him, even menacing. That was just my projection. His face could close up, alright, but when he felt safe and loved, Noah looked softer and more open than anyone I had ever known. Most of the people I knew had their armor up all the time, without the option of letting it go.

After the first bite, Noah passed his plate around and we all sampled the lobster. We savored a good white wine—our first contravening of the Family's rule against drugs. Conversation came easily, mostly travel stories—ours about people we had met on our film tour, theirs about a recent trip to Bulgaria to record traditional musicians. When, late in the evening, we went off to bed heavy with good food and wine, I felt content to have shared something with my companions that they might not have seen before—the wide world and artistic intelligence that I missed most when I ran away from academia.

Sometime in the middle of the night I woke up, lying on my back uncomfortably in the depression where the cushions met the back of the overstuffed couch. Someone was knocking at the window. I felt afraid, but safer when I realized I was not alone—Leanne and Arthur slept in an alcove on the other side of the room. I struggled through tangled bedding and knelt on the couch to look out. Through rain and leaves windblown against the glass I could see a man clinging somehow to the window frame and the downspout. It was Noah. I opened the window and he climbed in over the couch.

"I just went out for a walk," he whispered. "I had some things to think about. Then when I came back the house was dark, so. . . ." He grinned. I knew these old houses had overhangs and cornices and pillars and downspouts a person could climb. I hugged him with the cold air on my back.

"You go back to sleep," he said, pulling the window shut, and he tiptoed down the stairs.

In the morning I felt honored to have shared a secret with him.

"I'm glad it was you out there," I whispered to him.

He touched my shoulder and said, "I felt very close to you last night."

He felt close to me, and sex didn't have anything to do with it. This was a new kind of relationship for me. I had grown up so convinced that the main thing of value about me was my mind, and after that my sex, that I generally scanned any man primarily for signs that he was attracted to me—or not. And if he was, was I attracted to him? And if I was, were we going to have sex? This went for peers, professors, husbands of friends—all of them. That was what men were about. Feeling close to Noah, this big, gentle man with his helmet of kinky hair and his kind eyes, opened a whole new horizon of relationship.

On our second day in Seattle, I decided to visit my friend Isabel, an older woman who had studied with some of the fathers and mothers of American anthropology—Franz Boas, Cora Du Bois, Ruth Benedict— but had quit after the master's degree to marry an artist and pursue her deeper love, modern dance. Divorced after a stormy, and, I imagined, a romantic, bohemian life in San Francisco, she took a job at the University of Washington as the graduate student academic counselor.

I lived in her basement apartment early in my graduate career, when I had broken my ankle, had a cast up to my hip, and needed some mothering. She introduced me to egg blintzes for breakfast, to cooking with herbs, and to honesty in small things, such as the time I put tarragon in the scrambled eggs (at her suggestion), enough to turn them green (my interpretation), and she screamed, "My God, not that much." It was new to me that an older person could scream at me with such underlying good humor. In my family, you only screamed when you "lost control."

So I took the Mustang and drove north of the university to visit Isabel. She had recently married an old friend, a widower. They looked happy together. He was about a foot taller, an elegant, gray-haired man who curved toward her protectively as if he were about to embrace and lift her *en pointe*. They saw my joining the commune as a courageous political act, and she pressed a check for $25 into my hand as I was leaving.

"We'd be doing the same thing if we were younger," she said.

I felt like a charlatan. What we were doing seemed neither courageous nor political. I tried to give it back, but she insisted and I accepted it in the end.

When I returned to the house, Leanne told me that Arthur had phoned home to Taos, and found out that I was being sent to Iowa.

"Iowa? Whatever for?"

Byron had called from Iowa; he had arranged a showing at the University of Iowa but didn't have a copy of the film. Since we had two copies with us, he wanted me to get on a plane and bring him the extra one. I objected.

"It doesn't really take a person and a plane fare to get a copy of the film to Byron, does it?"

"No, but Byron wants to spend some time with you," Leanne said, her green eyes directed toward me with that now-familiar respect for the one being summoned.

"Oh." I had a sinking feeling, a ripple of excitement, and a confused sense that I would probably go.

She should not follow her whims

12 *Six in the second place means:*
She should not follow her whims.
She must attend within to the food.
Perseverance brings good fortune.

The wife must always be guided by the will of the master of the house,
be he father, husband, or grown son. Her place is within the house. There,
without having to look for them, she has great and important duties.

—*I Ching,* Chapter 37. *Chia Jen/*The Family

Byron waited for me outside the terminal, a solid, light-brown man in a
dark leather jacket, hands in his pockets, both feet planted firmly on the
ground. A cold wind blew wispy hair around the edges of his stocking
cap. His hazel eyes, smiling now, reminded me of my father's. He gave
me a light kiss, made softer by his missing front teeth. He took the film

canister and my suitcase from my hands, threw them on the back seat and headed around the car to the driver's side. I realized I was supposed to open the door for myself, and climbed in feeling foolish for hesitating.

On this day in late April, Persephone had not reached the flat Iowa fields. The landscape held little color. The river looked cold and gray, too—nothing I'd want to swim in. We drove into town to a motel near the University of Iowa. I wanted to go to a restaurant for dinner; Byron said he had some potato chips and Coke, and that would be enough.

"But it's not healthy to eat that kind of stuff for a meal," I said. "We need real food—vegetables and milk and meat."

"That's bullshit," Byron said, scowling. "People get hung up on that nutrition shit. It doesn't matter what you eat if you're really together. When you're spiritually high enough, you can make use of whatever you've got."

He didn't look like a yogi, but he didn't look unhealthy, either. His skin was smooth and brown, and his round body flexible and strong. I imagined a yogi sitting half-naked at the mouth of a modest cave, a bag of potato chips on the rock by his knee.

"That doesn't make sense to me," I said. The scowl deepened.

"Then you should trust me." He seemed to mean I should take anything he said as the gospel truth. But when food is involved, I get really serious. I'm hypoglycemic, although there wasn't a name for that condition at the time. All I knew was that I felt shaky, anxious, and irritable when I went for too long without food.

"Well, I'm not that together," I said. "At least we could get some stuff at a grocery store, couldn't we?"

Byron relented, drove me to a store, and waited while I went in.

Back at the motel I washed a couple of apples in the bathroom sink and sliced them up with my Swiss Army knife. Byron sat at the brown Formica-top table next to the window looking out on the parking lot. I offered him apples, cheese, and bread, which he accepted and seemed to enjoy as much as I did. I giggled. He grinned, and soon we were laughing. I got up to wash the knife and put away the food, and as I brushed past him he rested his hand on my waist, then let it slide down to caress my leg. I felt a little shiver of pleasure.

It's hard to remember this now, as I have nearly forgotten what it was like to be twenty-four and turned on by almost everything—by a man's touch, by the thought of sex, by an intellectual argument or a memory or by nothing at all but the feel of my own body beneath my clothes. And yet, in spite of that almost constant readiness, I still wasn't sure I could recognize an orgasm. In the midst of lovemaking, as my excitement built, I would moan and scream as evidence for my partner that he was doing a good job and I was coming. It seemed to work—at least for them.

That night, Byron interrupted my concert. He paused, curved over me in the dark. "Try to focus on that feeling without making any sound. Can you do that?" At first I felt a flash of anger. How dare he criticize me when I was just expressing myself? But I stifled a moan and felt something take over me as if my body were expanding and I was plunging wildly without any effort. He, too, shuddered and came, his arms wrapped around me, his hands twined in my hair and holding my head. After it was done he kissed my eyes and mouth softly, very softly, and we lay together limp and moist and gradually went to sleep.

The next morning I felt happy, even tender, and Byron, too, seemed relaxed. He agreed to a restaurant breakfast. I bought a local newspaper, but when I opened it and offered to share it, the scowl returned and he shook his head and looked out the window. I felt uncertain. Was he offended that I would read instead of talking to him? Did he just hate the mainstream propaganda of the newspapers? I didn't quite dare to ask, but instead skimmed the headlines and the comics uncomfortably until the waitress appeared with our food.

On the way back to the motel we passed a movie theater near the university and I saw that Luis Buñuel's *The Milky Way* was playing.

"Oh, wow," I said, "I love Buñuel. Let's go."

"I don't need entertainment," he said, his eyes on the traffic. "You go."

"But it's not an ordinary movie, it's an art film."

"Art is junk," he announced. Besides, it sounded too intellectual to him. "I don't think much. When I'm thinking it's because there's a problem."

He dropped me off for the matinee. The movie begins in an elegant dining room with a bizarre theological conversation between a maitre d' and waiters about the doctrine of the transubstantiation of the flesh. Criticism of the Catholic church, juxtaposition of characters and costumes from different centuries, the combination of the surreal, the intellectual, and the emotional, fascinated me. I thought the film was intensely relevant to the Family and wished Byron had seen it. I felt sure it would interest him, but he brushed off my attempt to tell him about it.

That night, Byron introduced our film to a small crowd in the Student Union auditorium and answered a few questions afterward. One or two earnest students stayed to talk with us; they had been thinking of starting a commune on farmland outside of town. The rest of the audience dispersed rather quickly.

As he packed the film into its canister, I broached a subject that had been on my mind for most of the film tour.

"Byron, have you noticed that a lot of people don't seem to get the point?"

"Yeah, we're too far out for most of them. But all we can do is put it in front of them and let them see what they're ready to see."

"But don't you think it might have something to do with some of the technical problems in the film? Maybe we should consider re-cutting it, or even re-doing some stuff." He looked up briefly, without much interest, and snapped the canister shut.

"No, I don't think so."

For him, the subject was closed. As it had been for the others when we heard much more direct criticism at the showing in Berkeley.

In Iowa City, Byron and I went back to the motel, made love again, and left the next morning for the next film showing in Athens, Ohio. Somewhere along the way I asked Byron if he wanted me to drive for a while.

"No, I can do it," he said.

"I know you can do it," I persisted. "Do you want me to drive for a while?"

He answered with a quick, dark glance, gripping the wheel more firmly.

"As long as I can do it, I'll do it," he said.

We arrived in the early afternoon and checked into a motel. After we had walked a few blocks to a cafe and had lunch, Byron took me back to the motel and busied himself pulling the drapes and turning on the TV.

"Don't you want to go out and look around town, explore a little, see what there is to do?" I asked. He looked at me blankly.

"No, I don't want to go out."

"But why not? We have almost three days here." I couldn't bear to think of holing up in a darkened motel room for three days. It sounded like prison.

"Didn't you see that man we passed on the way to the café?" he demanded. "Didn't you see how he looked at us?"

"Yeah, I saw it." The man's hostile stare had reminded me that we were in *southern* Ohio, and that Athens was a long way from Yellow Springs, the home of liberal Antioch College, and the only other Ohio town I had been in.

"If he had said anything to me about being with you I might have killed him. I don't want that to happen so I'm staying inside." He said this in the even tone of a father explaining a difficult subject to a child.

My breath stopped. I had no doubt that he could kill a person; he had a stocky build and looked powerful, and he must have had to be tough to survive his time in San Quentin. But the black men I had known in the past had been involved in the civil rights movement and the Southern Christian Leadership Conference. They hadn't talked like that. I had never known anyone who talked about killing people as if they meant it.

I said nothing, but the more I sat around with Byron, staring at the TV, the worse I felt—heavy and tight and churning with contradictions. He must be a bad person, I thought, to hold so much hate. And I'm white—he must hate me. But how would I cope with racism if I were black? It was wrong of me to judge him. But what about Martin Luther King and James Bevel and other leaders—they had reached deep within themselves and come up with a way to love their enemies, hadn't they? Or was that it? What did I know? Was it just that they used their anger— even hate—in a constructive way? And what about me? How could I be with a man who could kill people?

He sent out for pizza, we watched more TV, and then we went to bed. When he kissed and caressed me, I complied, but at the moment that he rolled over and vaulted on top of me, an explosion went off in my head. I pushed out at him, shoved him off, and cried, "What about me? Do you want to kill me, too?" It was dark. I could only see a quick move of astonishment as he pulled away, sat up, and turned on the light.

"My uncle's a racist. My mother's from the south. My people are the same as the ones walking around out there. What would you say if you met my relatives?"

The blood pounded in my head. I felt as though I was tearing myself apart, as though Byron would like to tear me apart, but he was sitting quietly among the tumbled bedclothes, watching my face.

Byron considered me, his brow slightly furrowed, his mouth a straight line.

"I'd really rather not," he said. "I already know what they're like."

Uncle Bubba would say the same. He would never want to meet Byron. To know the color of his skin and the fact that he had been in prison would be more than enough. Bubba, my mother's youngest brother and the darling of the family, was my favorite uncle when I was a little girl. He was built much like Byron; stocky, round-headed, with ham-like forearms and knees turned outward by his chunky thighs. He was great with kids; he could make eyes at a baby and get instant smiles. He used to lift us up on one hand toward the ceiling as we screamed with delight. His brothers and sisters could call on him in an emergency; he was the one who would stay calm, be competent, know what to do or how to fix it. My mother always said she wanted his to be the first face she would see when returning to consciousness after an operation.

Bubba was a soldier in China in the Second World War, then a cop in Detroit. We kids knew it was dangerous to wake him up—he might churn up out of sleep with his fists swinging. It was something about the war. But sitting around the kitchen table in the evening with a beer or a martini and a smoke, he could tell the best jokes and get everybody laughing, even Auntie Mil and Uncle Carl, or Uncle Ray and Aunt Caroline, the two married couples who seemed born to hate each other. His favorite jokes were told in dialect—the dialect of Amos 'n' Andy.

My father moved to California and my mother and I followed. Over the years, we saw my mother's family less and less. When we visited, I would get into arguments with Uncle Bubba about his racist jokes. As I became more articulate, the arguments grew more unpleasant. Finally, we stopped talking about anything other than family news. But he was still my uncle, and nothing could ever change that.

"I don't understand you," I sobbed. "I can't do this."

Byron sighed.

"All you have to do to get the freedom you want is take it," he said.

He switched out the light, made himself comfortable, and went to sleep.

The next morning he said he would put me on the plane to Albuquerque and take care of the film showing himself. On the drive to the airport, he told me that I was fucked up; that I couldn't trust anybody; and that I had better "find somebody I could trust or else burn out my mind." Those words stayed with me for a long time. Some years later I dreamed that the back of my head was hollowed out and stuffed with cotton, as if I had fulfilled his prophecy.

The family

13

Six in the fourth place means:
She is the treasure of the house.
Great good fortune.

It is upon the woman of the house that the well-being of the family
depends. Well-being prevails when expenditures and income are
soundly balanced. This leads to great good fortune. In the sphere of
public life, this line refers to the faithful steward whose measures fur-
ther the general welfare.

—*I Ching*, Chapter 37. *Chia Jen*/The Family

Approaching Albuquerque from the northeast, the plane drops over
Sandia Crest and glides across a great expanse, a landscape tilted into the
setting sun. The city, a bristling worm, crawls across this plain, but it can't
diminish the grandeur of the land and sky. Glad as I was to leave Byron,
I was twice as glad to return to New Mexico.

Daniel and James Joseph met me at the gate. Things at home, they told me, were getting a little tough, as there wasn't much money for the household. Those of us who were travelling had been using the "Lord Family" credit card, staying in motels and eating in restaurants, but nothing much was coming in to support the folks at home. The good news was that the local political scene had calmed down a little; there hadn't been any violent attacks against hippies in the last two weeks.

On the drive to Taos, the New Mexico landscape reasserted itself, awesome and harsh after Ohio. In such a short distance the land showed so many different faces: gentle cottonwoods meandering near the Rio Grande; the rocks shaped like Rubenesque thighs and shoulders near the turnoff to Dixon; the viewpoint from which the Rio Grande Gorge on the left and the high mountains to the right dwarf the town of Taos.

The pale green chamisa along the road to the house looked fluffy; perhaps it would blossom soon. The willows and cottonwoods to the west along the river had noticeably greened up in the two weeks I was gone. The Family's rented adobe, with its grayed wooden doorways and crowded interior, smelled faintly of sandalwood incense, rotting lettuce, and recent baking. Lady April had made bread. She was the only one at home, and she was moving slowly—calmer, tanner, and even bigger in the belly, ready to pop any day now. I emptied my suitcase, returning my travelling clothes to the cut-loose box and Leanne's corner of the closet, and put the suitcase under April's bed. This time the house seemed familiar, and not having any personal space felt fine, almost cozy. Better than being alone in a motel room with Byron.

I spent the next day hanging around at home. There wasn't much to do, but I didn't have a role at the General Store or the Day Care Center and didn't much want one. Every time someone mentioned Byron, I tensed. April asked me how I had enjoyed my time with him.

"I had a fight with him," I said. She looked surprised.

"Once you get to know him better I'm sure you'll love him. He's really far out."

In the afternoon Lady Maya was sunning herself out in the yard. I sat down next to her and stretched out my legs to get some tan. She looked lush, steamy, like a tropical plant, not at all dry from the high desert sun. Her dark, wavy hair curled at her temples.

"How was your trip with Byron?" she asked.

"Everyone else seems to love Byron," I said, "but I think I hate him." She looked at me curiously. I flushed. I felt self-conscious under her gaze.

"Do you love him too?" I asked. She smiled and looked down, sorting through her feelings.

"Yes, I'm in love with that man," she said in a musky voice, "that man who gives me so much trouble. I stayed at the Gallery House last month to be near him, after he moved into town. He's always stronger than I am, more in touch with now, more really here."

More really here. I heard that so much in the Family. The essence of Gestalt therapy is to be fully present. More neo-Freudian than anti-Freudian, Perls demonstrated that all the childhood conflicts, the fears and angers and pains that constitute neurosis can be found in the present experience and the relationships happening right now. Don't ask why, he said, and spend years analyzing yourself looking for the answer; ask how—how am I making myself angry, fearful, or happy, right now? How am I being in the world right now? All the answers are here.

Perls defined neurosis as a kind of rigidity, the inability to allow experience to move through, transform, and move on. Neurosis is being stuck because you cannot allow yourself to feel what you feel, or to be what, in this moment, you truly are. I had read Perls. I believed in this process. I did not, however, have the faintest notion how to apply it to myself. I felt sure that Maya knew something I did not know and that Byron, if she said so, also had a mysterious quality beyond my reach.

"He used to stay with me in my house up in Arroyo Seco," she said dreamily. "I wasn't in the Family then. But after a while he said, 'I can't get caught in this, I love a lot of people, not just one,' and I understood that. Even though it wasn't what I wanted. But I accepted it and I was okay with it. Once he brought another girl into the room next to mine and slept with her." Maya shrugged her tan, rounded shoulders. "It really freaked her out more than me."

This story hit me like a body blow. She really loved him. They spent time alone together. He must have felt close to giving in to her, to losing something. I remembered his voice, harsh and abrupt, in a Gestalt session focused on Leanne and George: "Marriage is just a way for a woman to get control of a man."

And yet Maya accepted the change when he pulled away from her,

accepted the premise that she must loosen up, let go of him, even acqui-
esce in a meditative, calm state as he fucked someone else in a room next
to her where she could hear them. I recognized the implication; she had
achieved a spiritual pinnacle, a Family ideal. I felt somehow horrified, or
frightened, or upset in the stomach; feelings I couldn't look at too closely,
and so I said "far out" and got up and walked away.

Byron put the same principle into practice for others in the Family,
not just for himself. He separated close couples if he thought it was best
for the group. In a long telephone call from Ohio, Byron decided to go
from there to New York, to join with George and some others working
on marketing the film and raising more money through grants. Byron
asked Isabel to join him. I was surprised to hear that Isabel was going to
New York without Daniel.

Why? I asked Leanne another day, as we sat side by side on a wooden
box in the yard, watching her daughter, Gina. In the back of my mind I
was aware that, theoretically, I was just as responsible as Leanne for this
child's well-being, but I wasn't paying much attention. Gina wore nothing but short white pants, and she was muddling around by the fence
pulling up dry stalks of grass.

"Oh, Byron thinks they're just too tight and they ought to spend
less time together," Leanne said. Gina rambled over and tickled Leanne's
face with the grass. Leanne pulled her up onto her lap and wrapped her
arms around Gina's pale chest. I wondered if she wasn't cold; although
it was almost the first of May, the wind still carried a chill from the mountains.

"Really? But why? They're so happy together. It looks like they love
each other." This visible closeness awed me. I had never experienced a
long-term, comfortable, loving relationship. Mine had been passionate,
stormy, and, above all, short.

"That's why they're doing it," she said, turning to look at me, all
green-eyed and solemn. "Maybe you haven't gotten this yet. We're prac-
ticing these long separations in order to break up any special bonds we
have with just one other person. A tight couple takes energy away from
the group."

"Far out," I managed.

She nodded wisely. "One person's death can't stop the functioning
of the whole."

"But what about parents and children? Like what about you and Gina? You wouldn't want to leave her, would you?"

"No, I wouldn't." Her eyes widened and she looked away. "I would do anything for her." Gina, unconcerned, bobbled her foot against her mother's knee. "I cried every night we were on the road with the film. But that was the reason Byron sent me away. He wanted me to know that other people could take care of her just as good as me."

This gave me a sinking feeling. I remembered a recent hassle in which four angry women gave William a tongue-lashing for allowing Laura's baby to fall off the couch while he was sitting right next to it. I felt sure William wouldn't have hurt the baby deliberately, but the baby got hurt, and he didn't seem to feel responsible.

I felt hungry. It was mid-afternoon, and we had had pancakes for breakfast and pancakes for lunch. I left Leanne holding her toddler and went inside, looking for a snack. A piece of cheese would have been nice, or some yogurt, or even some fruit or bread. The refrigerator held left-over pancake batter, two eggs, and half a head of iceberg lettuce. Nothing to snack on, and nothing for dinner, either. From there I went looking for April, who was in charge of the household budget when Isabel was gone. April was at the General Store, Heather told me, getting some supplies.

But lately there hadn't been much money for anything at home, not even food. The folks who were travelling had the Family credit card, as we had while we were on the film tour, but we couldn't use that at home. No one had listened to Lorraine, the bookkeeper, when she said there was no money left to take the movie on the road. They were sure that once we got it out there, some major distributor would pick it up and we'd have plenty of money. But the film showings had just barely paid for themselves, mainly because people had put us up for free at nearly all of the stops. Lorien Foundation had gone bust, and there wasn't any other money coming in. We had great credit, after spending the $20,000 grant. The general feeling was that since "money is just energy," why not spend the credit?

Unfortunately, the "energy" being spent on the credit card was other people's—people we knew and had to deal with in person in Taos. Creditors called frequently, particularly the local businesses to whom we owed thousands of dollars; letters from collection agencies piled up;

occasionally someone showed up at the Gallery House to make the case for paying them. At first these visits were polite, but they became increasingly unpleasant.

Lorraine, Philip, and Adam, who had little weight in the Family, finally convinced Daniel, Christopher, and Noah to talk to "Control" in New York. Byron and George stonewalled them. They would get a breakthrough any day now; we should tough it out. The argument went on for a week, as the phone bill climbed past a thousand dollars. Lorraine left the Family; Philip refused to handle the books any longer; and Adam, an odd, lumpy fellow who had never done much to distinguish himself, volunteered to take them over. While the three in New York stayed in a hotel and ate in good restaurants, thanks to the credit card, at home food got scarce.

April brought home rice and beans from the General Store and we managed a tasty meal that night. The next day I went into town and started looking for a job. A local photographer was advertising for a part-time assistant. I found his studio on a dusty back street in a wooden building that look abandoned. The display window hadn't been washed for a few seasons. I could barely make out some sepia-toned wedding photos and a few interesting portraits of local people. Mr. Rudolph looked as though he had lived in his darkroom for about forty years, but he was nice enough, and I took the job. He needed help with retouching. I sat for hours in dim light with a tiny brush, erasing moles, wrinkles, and blotches of developer. It was kind of fun—at least it made me feel competent. My mother had always gone out and gotten a job when she needed to. Here, the women at home seemed to find my behavior strange, and perhaps a little admirable, but nobody else followed suit.

I gave my wages to April. It took only $100 a week to feed our thirty to fifty people; but now we didn't even have that much to spend. The women had a meeting and decided we would have to take Janine out of the Montessori school because we couldn't afford the tuition.

With Isabel in New York, Daniel and I had been spending a lot of time together. He missed her, and it showed in the way he moved sometimes, restless and sharp instead of with his usual grace. But nothing seemed to get him down for long. Hard times didn't seem to bother him; he had a light touch with everything. When he led the Gestalt sessions they turned funny instead of accusing. Daniel and Noah, whom I trusted absolutely since getting to know him on the film tour, loved each other like real brothers. They both grew up in Oakland and had been in the Family from the start.

One morning I encountered Daniel sitting against the adobe wall of the house with his face turned to the sun, eyes closed; he looked relaxed and benign, and he glowed like a gold-leafed icon. On the way into town, I told him he looked like the Golden Sun Buddha. He laughed, jouncing around in the back of the van, half-standing over me. "Well, I think you're wonderful," he said. Wonderful? That set off a sunburst inside me, a bright tingle of joy.

A hippie couple travelling in their van stopped by and asked to stay for a few days. They brought in some food to share, and apologetically laid two tomatoes, an avocado, and some carrots on the kitchen table. Daniel, April and I stared. We hadn't had vegetables for at least a week. The head count was down to about twenty at the house, still too many to get more than a taste of these precious foods. Daniel grinned around the toothpick he seemed to be chewing on a lot these days and asked if I wanted to help him look for more vegetables for dinner.

"Sure, but what?"

"Wild asparagus." He grabbed a burlap bag from the pantry and headed out the front door. It had rained a trace; the wind carried the sweet, sharp smell of earth and creosote.

"It should be easy to spot," Daniel said. "It's a tall, feathery plant. I'm sure I've seen some out here." We scuffed through cheat grass and tumbleweeds, scanning across the field for subtle green stalks. A magpie flipped off the barbed wire fence and flew out toward the road. Horsetail cirrus clouds brushed the sky over toward the Taos Pueblo. After fifteen minutes of searching we found a modest patch of asparagus across the way, near the fence line. Daniel crouched before it and pawed around. He found three stalks. I put them in the bag. By the time we had covered the field and returned to the house we had five. Five slender green fingers to provide vitamins for twenty people. We steamed them, chopped them, and put them in a salad with the gifts from our guests.

The shooting at the hot springs, before we left on the film tour, had marked the peak of the violence between locals and hippies, but tension stayed high. Narinda Baker, a local art gallery owner, wanted to do something about the social divisions within the town. She decided to throw a party to bring together some friends of hers from "the Establishment" and some hippies. She called the General Store. Daniel accepted the invitation on behalf of the Family.

Narinda and her husband, Doug, had moved to Taos from their hometown in west Texas. While he ran a ranch to the north of town, she painted local scenes—Taos Pueblo, fall colors, the river canyon—and had developed a fine reputation. She bought an old adobe building on a side street near the plaza and remodeled it herself to make her gallery. She was well liked, and well positioned to make a conciliatory move.

Daniel asked me to go with him to Narinda's. Leanne offered me a rose-and-green floral party dress from her mysterious private stock. It felt like a date, maybe the most exciting date of my life.

"You really like him, don't you?" Leanne said. I hugged her.

Daniel drove me into town in the Mustang. I kissed his ear, his neck, his cheek, and he laughed and turned up the radio and we sang, "Take another little piece-a my heart now, babee."

Narinda's house was an old adobe on one of the good streets east of the plaza. We crunched through dry leaves on the stone walkway, and before we could knock, the door opened. Narinda, in a bright aquamarine dress with a full skirt, dangly earrings, and cowgirl boots, drawled, "Ha. C'mawn in." She looked about forty, tall and plain, with her long brown hair in a ponytail, but she had a nice figure and a good sense of western style. In the cavelike entry, I smelled cool earth and sage, overlaid with party scents—chips and dips, perfume, red wine. She pulled us into a circle of well-dressed middle-aged couples. Narinda told us we had to learn all we could about each other and we should be "real honest and open."

Doug handed us a couple of beers—Coors, ubiquitous in Colorado and New Mexico. A pink-faced older man with eyebrows like wild bunchgrass pulled a stick of beef jerky out of his pocket, grinned, and offered me a bite.

"This is Stanley Jameson, a local artist," Doug said. "and you are?"

"I'm Daniel and this is Lily," Daniel said. "We're from the Family"

"The Family?" Jameson echoed. Apparently we weren't the household word I thought we were.

"Yeah, we're kind of the social workers of the Taos hippie scene," Daniel said. "We run the General Store, the Information Center, and the

Free Clinic. Just trying to help the kids who come here expecting life to be easy."

"And do you have some particular principle or focus for your group?" Doug asked.

"We're a group marriage," Daniel said. "We use Gestalt therapy to help everybody grow up and get along."

Jameson's eyebrows shot up like chamisa in the wind. He fastened on me.

"Group marriage? What's that all about? Orgies?"

"No," I began earnestly. "It's not like that. That's just a stereotype. It's really about commitment."

A fortyish woman, resplendent in turquoise earrings and a heavy silver squash-blossom necklace, captured Daniel and grilled him about hippie morals. What did he think about hippies sunbathing naked in public in this conservative Catholic community?

"In the Family we're careful about that," Daniel said. "We're trying to calm everybody down."

She crossed her arms and studied him, taking in his clear dark eyes, copper skin, white teeth, and easy, relaxed-cat stance.

"We've made a commitment to the community," he went on, and "we really want to get along with the local people. That's why we started the Information Center. Anybody stopping in there gets a lecture about local customs and staying cool with the local folks."

"Hm, I see," the woman said, uncrossing her arms and smiling back at him. Mr. Big Eyebrows was on his own track, though, waving his glass of whiskey and pushing his white-shirted paunch closer to me, ignoring Daniel.

"But don't you have sex with anybody you want to?" he insisted. His manner was flirtatious, but I wasn't offended. I thought he really wanted to know.

"Well, yeah," I said. "If *they* want to, too. Don't you?" He burst out laughing.

"Touché," he said, and backed off.

I looked around at the living room of whitewashed adobe. A large painting of the Taos Pueblo in soft blues and browns hung over the fireplace. Cushions along the white denim couch and the Navajo rug in the center of the floor echoed the turquoise, brown, black, and accents of dusty rose that Narinda favored. The entire room had texture; no table or chair brought in square corners or sharp edges to fracture the feeling of refuge and comfort. Narinda saw my scrutiny, took my arm and steered me around the room.

"This place used to belong to a friend of D. H. Lawrence," she said. "The walls and the *vigas* are the same as they were then." I asked about a humble-looking brown stick bound with leather and fringed with mottled feathers that hung on the back wall. It didn't seem to fit with the rest of the furnishings.

"That's a very powerful object," Narinda drawled, looking at me intently. "An Indian friend of mine, a medicine woman, gave that to me." I was impressed that Narinda had Indian friends.

"How do you know it's a power object?"

"It's just a feeling," she said. She held her hands a foot apart as if she were holding something that was vibrating. "You just feel the energy."

I could hear Daniel explaining something about our concept of twenty-four-hour encounter to Doug.

"Hey everybody . . ." A woman in pink, one of the realtors, overcome with good feeling, raised her voice to take in the whole room. "Let's all sit here in a circle and *do it.*" It wasn't at all clear what we were supposed to do, but she kept at it, smiling and waving vaguely, and somehow got about ten people sitting on the floor cross-legged, holding their drinks and looking expectant.

"This is it," she told us. "Let's be real open and honest, like Narinda said. Let's talk about the problems we've got in our town and see if we can figure out what to do about 'em." By that time enough alcohol had been consumed to loosen tongues and blur memories. I don't remember much more of what was said, but I do know we had a good time. The party broke up around midnight with plenty of loud, happy "see you soons" and quite a few hugs. I felt proud to have shared the night with Daniel.

"I want to stay with you tonight," he whispered as we were leaving, and squeezed my hand. I was floating in an exquisite high from the conversation and the excitement and pride of being with him. We drove to the Gallery House and made love in the solitude of an upstairs room. I felt an urgency that he seemed to meet, an excitement that was more than sexual, as if our bodies and souls had agreed about what we were doing and where we were going. This level of intimacy was new to me. I felt overwhelmed at the thought that this beautiful man actually loved me. The next morning we went back to the house at Llano and I imagined that the eyes upon me were respectful in a new way; that I was being seen as I really was, and I really was loving and being loved back by Daniel.

I realized Daniel had a deep commitment to Isabel, with whom he had fathered Amos, now only about a year old, and that he missed her intensely. Nevertheless, knowing this, I thought that Daniel was in some sense mine. A day or two after the party, sitting with him in the school bus, I said something to that effect. In fact, here's exactly what I said: "I want to tell the world you're mine." We had been nuzzling, telling silly secrets, basking in each other's smiles. With those words, the warmth faded from his eyes. The school bus might as well have started up its motor and driven over a cliff; he couldn't have tumbled away from me any faster.

"That's disgusting," he said. "You can't possess me." I sat there staring at him. "You've got to know me on my own terms, in my own time."

"But . . . I just said what I thought. I don't even know what I meant."

"Well, I don't like it." He got up and left me sitting alone in the bus, like a fish in a dumpster.

The next day Noah asked me what was going on with me. I started to cry.

"Daniel's mad at me," I blubbered, expecting sympathy.

"Well," Noah answered, with a neutral expression, "I can sure understand that after what you said."

"You mean Daniel told you that? I can't believe he would tell you such a personal thing."

"We have no secrets in the Family," he admonished. "Nothing you say, nothing about you is private here. If you say it to Daniel it's the same as saying it to me."

The enormity of this stunned me. Words whispered between lovers? Intimate moments in bed? My sins—the fact that I could be possessive. It was actually legitimate to be betrayed.

"God, I hate that," I wailed.

6-3-70

Dear Marion,

We talked to Margaret last night—has she written you anything about this commune near Taos? And this trip she made to Seattle & back? Her present address is Box 190 Arroyoseco New Mexico 87514. Apparently it is a decent group, with a vision and energy along rational lines, but—?? Punker and Norma (who thinks that "therapy" M. had is responsible) don't mesh too well. N. is with the Eisenhower Medical Center now and is well situated.

. . . your everlovin' brother

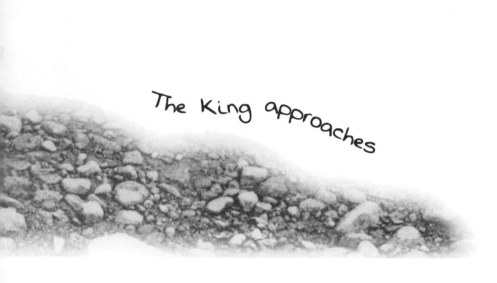

The King approaches

14

Nine in the fifth place means:
As a king he approaches his family.
Fear not.
Good fortune.

A king is the symbol of a fatherly man who is richly endowed in
mind. He does nothing to make himself feared; on the contrary, the
whole family can trust him, because love governs their intercourse.
His character of itself exercises the right influence.

—*I Ching*, Chapter 37. *Chia Jen*/The Family

Spring is a dry season in northern New Mexico, but the low-growing
things that give this land its texture—the rabbit brush, chamisa, Indian
grass, even the sage—still take their mysterious turnings into bloom. In
early June a warm wind blew across the Llano Quemado, ruffling yellow
flowers of rabbit brush, the subtle fluff of chamisa, the tassels of Indian

grass, and tiny, waxy white clusters on the sage. I took a morning walk
along the road toward the highway, sniffing the breeze and flinging my
arms around just to feel free. Here on the ridge the world looked wide
indeed.

Up ahead I saw the Family's white van turn in from the highway.
Thomas stopped long enough to exchange smiles. He looked healthy and
ruddy, his straight red hair smoothed back, and he wore a multicolored
tie-dye T-shirt that picked up the blue in his eyes. He was quite handsome and I told him so. We both laughed.

"Hey, I got the news from Daniel at Control," he said. "They're
coming home tomorrow." I felt the blood drain out of my face. Byron,
George, and Isabel were coming home from New York.

"Oh," I said.

"Daniel's sure happy. Everybody'll be glad to see them."

"Does it mean they're giving up on getting money for the film?"

"I don't know. Ask George when he gets here."

God, I thought, George is the last person I'd ask anything. The
home crew must have finally won the argument about money. Daniel
would have Isabel again, and that would draw the line under our distance.
And Byron would suck the air out of my world. I smiled again weakly
and Thomas drove off. He wasn't into mindfucking—if he saw my mood
change, he didn't need to bore into it.

I sat down on a rock by the side of the road and hugged my knees.
Now all I could see was the crumbly dirt and my own square toes poking
out of my sandals. I felt inert. Road kill. Byron a massive boulder block-
ing off my life, a control freak who had control. No space in my heart,
tight chest, tight throat. I'd have to get out. But if I left, I'd lose my gentle
friends, Thomas, Leanne, Noah, Arthur, even Daniel, no longer a lover,
but still so dear. If I stayed I would have to live with Byron and George
and the crazy ups and downs they would put us through. But Fritz Perls
was right, I couldn't stay contracted forever, I had to exhale. Eventually
I stood up and walked back to the house.

Thomas had brought the mail from town and had left a letter for
me on the kitchen table. It was from my father, scribbled, as always, and
hard to read. He and my stepmother were back from their trip to clear
out the cottage and complete its sale. She had had hand surgery and was
recovering.

6-12-70

Hi Sugar Bun:

We were in Los Angeles Tuesday to the doctor and Elvera's paws are get-ting along OK. Still soaks them 3X a day. I will probably still haul up her girdle for her and do other chores that require finger strength, for a while. We came back from Hemet Monday and stopped at a new orchard in Beaumont—had very fine cherries, so I picked 10 lbs. Wish you could enjoy them.

Re the enclosed check, I am getting this $100 every month from Pete Stanley on the cottage sale, and think you should have it as a backstop each month.

We stayed over Wednesday in L.A. & saw Zorba at the Pavilion— very good and rather unusual.

Much love, more later—Dad

P.S. I wonder sometimes about your living arrangements and security con-ditions—so if you don't get this by Monday let me know right away. XXXX

I put the check in my pocket.

In the kitchen, Noah and Leanne were making beans and rice, argu-ing and laughing about how much chili powder to put in the beans. He swooped a heaping-full serving spoon over the pot and she pushed his hand away, shrieking that he was a maniac. She played the fishwife well. He had an indulgent look as he knocked about half the lava-colored stuff into the sink and aimed again at the pot, waiting for a reaction. I knew that he loved her loud mouth. In situations where his instinct was to close down and watch and wait, hers would be to attack with words, to pummel and slash in her working-class English accent.

I remembered Noah's face, dark and open and laughing, as he stood one day in the kitchen door and teased me—I don't remember the con-tent of it, but it was some kind of teasing threat. I clung to his arm, but I felt like a little kid clinging to its father's pants leg. I felt as if I were on the floor raising my arms up to him, and I had an absolute certainty that he wouldn't hurt me.

"So this is trust," I thought, as if the word had no content before, like Helen Keller learning the name for water as she felt it running over her hand.

I sat down at the kitchen table and Leanne turned from the stove, looked at me and asked what was wrong.

"I got a letter from my father," I said. "It made me want to go home."

"Home? This is home."

"Not for me."

Noah stirred the beans, put the spoon down and came over to me.

"You've been lookin' pretty down lately," he said.

My stomach growled. I had been having intestinal cramps for a few days. *Down* wasn't quite the word. I felt as though I was being chainsawed. These people I loved—even feisty Leanne—all seemed willing to let Byron and George make their decisions for them. It was useless to try to form an alliance against them, and I knew I would lose if I faced either one of them alone. Byron was stronger and George was meaner than anyone else here.

"Yeah, I just don't know what to do."

Cynthia, a hard-faced little woman, looked into the room, sniffed out the presence of emotion, and came in to add her two cents. She sat down at the table across from me.

"I hope you'll stay," Leanne said. "Straight people are *nowhere*. Mike Szabo is your friend . . ." (She had been impressed during our stay in Seattle.) "but even he wouldn't stick by you like we do, and keep going back to you over and over to find out where you're at."

Actually, Mike did offer support sometimes when I was feeling bad. In a quick move on the way to class or standing behind his office door, he would look me over, his dark eyes moist, cup my cheek in his hand and ask in a husky voice, "What's wrong, little bird?"

"He used to do that," I said, thinking that the way he did it felt intrusive, hokey, even though it seemed to be kind.

"Then maybe he should be here," Leanne said. What an odd thought. Mike, on the rise in his academic career, joining a hippie commune? My rejection probably showed on my face. Noah pointed out that Mike had a lot of alternatives.

"Well, I have alternatives, too," I said. "I can't stay here just because I have no place to go. I do have places. Lots of places."

"Then maybe you should go to them," Leanne said. "I would be nothing without the Family. We are the misfits. This is the only place for us to be."

"I am not a misfit. I will not be a misfit," I said.

Leanne's green eyes held my gaze. She remained solemn, unoffended, and patient. "Well, maybe this will help you find out what you are."

Cynthia weighed in.

"You are one of the densest people I've ever met," she said. "You're totally unaware of what's going on."

What a bitch. I never felt comfortable around her. She looked pinched and worn, and whenever she noticed me, contemptuous.

"That's not true," I declared hotly, calmly, "that's not true."

But my body seemed to be trying to tell me something. As I left the kitchen, my stomach hurt, my bowels churned, my nose was running, my sinuses ached, and I felt wretched. It didn't feel like flu; it felt like a warning.

The next day I went to my job at the photographer's studio and sat listlessly touching up photos. I decided to take a break and walk over to see Narinda. She was in her office at the back of the gallery, taping up a shipment of paintings. She looked cheerful and clean, the western businesswoman in a fringed leather skirt and vest and a blue shirt with mother-of-pearl buttons. All she lacked was the cowgirl hat, but I had no doubt it was hanging on a nail somewhere nearby.

"Ha, Lily," she drawled, "Har yew?"

I wasn't too good. I complained for a while about my various physical woes. She asked how it was going at the Family. I told her I was dreading the return of Byron and George to Taos.

"Which one's George?" she asked. "Was he the guy who kept tryin' to get Doug and me to join?"

I thought he was. I remembered seeing Doug and George talking for a while when I had invited Narinda's family over for dinner. It looked like the classic encounter between expressive culture and whatever the opposite is—northern European inexpressive culture? George was gesturing, Doug wasn't. George was leaning in, Doug was moving back. George was doing his best to persuade and involve, while Doug looked like someone who happened to walk by the lot but had no intention of buying a car.

"George seemed to want to get Doug's skills in there for your group."

"You mean like ranching skills?" This seemed unlikely. Surely George wasn't thinking of getting the Family into ranching. We were an urban bunch, used to renting houses, not owning them, and moving on without building anything. Maybe George wanted Doug's business acumen. That would be ironic, given the Family's nonchalance about spending other people's money.

"He wanted us all to join—me and the kids, too. Doug thought it over for a while. He kinda liked the idea."

"What about you, Narinda? Would you want to join the Family?"

"Heavens, no!" she laughed, jangling her earrings. "I love my privacy. Look at me—I'm living in town while Doug and the boys are out there on the ranch. I would never join a commune."

She had a family—a real family. She had her passion, her art. Both seemed remote, unattainable, and extremely attractive to me. It was one of those things that others seemed to manage easily. But not for me. Narinda finished taping up a large, flat box and put down her scissors and tape.

"Lily, what's your problem? It's not just the flu."

I said that sometimes I wanted to leave the Family but I wasn't sure what to do or where I would go. She looked earnestly into my eyes.

"You can stay at my house whenever you want."

The horizon opened up briefly. But at that moment, I wasn't sure it would help to have a place to stay. It doesn't really matter, I told myself. In the cosmic perspective, it doesn't really matter. I thanked her and went back to work.

In the late afternoon, I rode home in the van with the others from the General Store. The Mustang was parked in front of the house when we arrived, and I knew Daniel and Thomas had taken it to Albuquerque to meet the plane. Byron was home. I stumbled getting out of the van. It was suddenly hard to breathe.

I walked in through the kitchen and saw Daniel in the Green Room with Isabel on his lap. He looked the way I remembered him from before, his face relaxed in a golden, Buddha-like calm. She was truly his mate. He looked at peace with himself, no longer the restless young hustler I saw in him sometimes while she was gone. I circled around through the other bedrooms and hovered in the doorway behind them.

George, commanding attention in the center of the room, bragged in a raucous voice that he had signed a contract to show the film on German television.

"Far out, man," Daniel said, always generous with his approval, his arm around Isabel's waist, his hand on her belly.

Byron raised his eyebrows at Thomas to signal that he was ready to go into town, and the two of them went out through the kitchen.

"It would be cool to have a ceremony tonight to give everybody their new titles," April said. Daniel and Isabel nodded.

"New titles?" I murmured.

"Yeah," Noah said, "there's a bunch of you people that joined about the same time that should get titles now. And I think Laura and Richard are gonna be promoted."

After dinner, Thomas came back to take us into town. We were down to about twenty members now, considerably diminished from the abundance of food and company two months before when we celebrated our New Age Passover and Kenneth was declared king.

Early stars dotted the sky, still a mysterious midnight blue to the west over the Rio Grande, dark over Taos Mountain. No other cars moved along the narrow, winding street by the Gallery House. It looked vacant—a tall, round-shouldered castle waiting for servants to light the lamps. As others prepared the room for another ceremony, turning on lights, finding the candles, pushing the table aside, Byron came up to me and said hello. I answered but turned aside.

"Lily," he admonished me, "Remember; find out why you hate me." I glanced away. My stomach burned.

The women had set the dais with candles, and Daniel called everybody together. Byron easily slipped into his public persona, almost a Will Rogers aw-shucks t'ain't-nothin'-special routine with a curly smile. He started off with some easy hellos, said it had been a good trip and he was glad to be home and see us all together again.

"Some people have earned new titles," he went on, standing up straighter, drawing back his shoulders, putting on a serious look, "and I will hereby confer them. Stanley, please come before me." Stanley, who had joined about the same time I had, and who still slept in the living room, worked his way to the front and stood facing Byron. Byron put his hands on Stanley' shoulders, and gently pushed down.

"Kneel." Stanley, in confusion, knelt.

Byron stretched out his hand, patted Stanley's head, and said, "I dub thee Sir Stanley. Rise, Sir Stanley."

Everyone cheered. As Sir Stanley returned to his seat, William and Kenneth rose up to hug him.

"Good job, man! Congratulations, man!" Even golden April pressed him to her perfect breasts and pregnant belly, then patted him on the cheek. Stanley took it all in with a hangdog grin.

Byron called William before him, transformed him into Sir William by the same procedure, and then made Mistress Laura a Lady, and Sir Richard a Lord. Then it was my turn.

"Lily, please come before me."

Byron waited on the dais in the candlelight, and a few eyes turned toward me. In this truly awful moment I realized I could no longer suspend disbelief. Whatever meaning this drama had for others, it didn't have for me. I felt incapable of responding, and terrified not to. If I refused to go up there, I would surely be condemned and humiliated. That part of me that was still eleven years old and the new kid, feeling the eyes of the class upon me as I walked to the front of the room, or the eyes of the boys as I carried my lunch tray to a table, or the eyes of the girls in P.E. as I flubbed the volleyball—that eleven year old could not bear to shatter this crystalline agreement and simply refuse Lord Byron's call. But the part that was twenty-five felt like a dog with its leg in a trap, utterly captured and debased by taking part in this idiotic charade.

I rose and walked forward to be beheaded. I bowed down without quite kneeling, and Byron's hand came down on my head.

"I dub thee Mistress Lily. Rise, Mistress Lily." I didn't look at him. All I saw was his round torso, dark leather jacket, and the flickering light.

"Fuck this," I thought. "It's crazy bullshit." But in my own insanity, I hated the "mistress" part the most. I'm a lady, I wanted to shout, a lady or nothing. A misfit, a loser. What was I doing there? As I crept back toward the darkest end of the room I heard clapping. Samantha stood to hug me.

"You've come a long way, Lily," she whispered in my ear. "You're really with us." How could Samantha be so far off? I sat down on the floor blinded with shame and rage. The ceremony continued.

"We are becoming the organism of many who act as one," Byron intoned. "We cannot hide anything from each other."

"I have nothing to hide," came Daniel's voice. "Nor have I," "Nor I." Murmured assents came from across the room, in back of me, beside me; no one had anything to hide.

I did. I saw a naked emperor up there—but I was afraid to speak. Face burning, heart thumping, I sat hunched over on the floor in the dark.

When it was finally over I rode back to the house in the press of bodies in the Chevy van and crawled into my lower bunk.

Perhaps I was crazy. Everybody else liked all this, loved Byron, took the ceremony seriously. What was wrong with me? But my body told a different story; I ached, belched, itched, snuffled, choked, and got the message. I really must leave. I couldn't fight it.

In the morning, I called Narinda.

"Do you want me to come get you?"

"Yes," I said. "Please."

I pulled my suitcase out from under the bed in the Yellow Room and fished a few of my clothes from the cut-loose box. April moved slowly in from the Green Room and tucked her head down to sit on the lower bunk across from me. She settled in with a sigh, her hands holding her belly as if she were trying to carry the baby in her arms. I told her I was leaving, and I was going to stay with Narinda in town. She didn't seem surprised, but I had never seen anything disturb her tranquil surface.

"I'm glad you have a place to crash," she said, neutral but kind.

I felt ashamed to get my sleeping bag out of the bus with April watching, and decided to leave the sleeping bag behind. My camera and purse, however, were still mine, and so was my toothbrush. As I closed the suitcase, Kenneth approached, and grabbed me in a tight embrace, which I endured. He released me and peered into my eyes, with an anxious monkey grimace.

"I really love you very much," he said. His eyes glittered behind their round, black frames.

"I know, but I don't love you." I turned away.

"Haven't you ever loved anyone who didn't love you in return?" he asked, and grabbed my arm and bent over and started kissing it like a leper. I pulled back my arm.

William came in to say goodbye and hugged me to his bulk. He had joined the Family shortly before I did; we shared the mattresses on the living room floor for a few days, and I remembered my revulsion at the thought of having sex with him. But that was only my thought, not his. He had offered his friendship in an innocent, straightforward way that eventually went to my heart. I would always remember William.

Sean wasn't around, to my relief, since the last thing I wanted was another probing, accusing Gestalt. Samantha was in town at the Gallery House, and I wouldn't have a chance to say goodbye to her. I felt sad to leave without ever knowing her. Maya would also remain in my memory as a mystery, a feminine seer, and I would never understand just what it was that she could see.

George walked through the living room, glanced at me and paused long enough to tell me I'd be back. "Fuck you," I thought, and looked away. And there was Richard, my archetypal lover, dark-haired, handsome, and articulate as a brick. I'd probably forget Richard. Finally, Narinda pulled into the yard, and Leanne and Daniel walked me out to her truck.

"Remember," Leanne said, "you can always come back. Once a member of the Family, always a member of the Family." She hugged me, and then Daniel hugged me. I pressed my face into the warm hollow of his neck and breathed in the clean smell of his skin.

"Remember," Daniel said, "I'm always here for you. If you need me you can call on me, and you can call on my brothers, Noah, and James Joseph, and Thomas, and Byron, and they will all be there for you the same as me."

I threw my suitcase in the back of Narinda's truck and climbed in. As we rattled out of the yard and up the road I looked back at the house, almost the same color as the earth in the dried-out field.

Under heaven thunder rolls

15 *We cannot lose what really belongs to us, even if we throw it away. Therefore we need have no anxiety. All that need concern us is that we should remain true to our own natures and not listen to others.*

—*I Ching*, Chapter 25. *Wu Wang*/Innocence (the Unexpected)

A "power object" similar to the one in Narinda's living room hangs over the bed in the guest room, a dim adobe cave with a small window set into the foot-thick wall. It's only a stick, with some feathers bound with leather—or perhaps sinews?—but Narinda speaks of it as if it could protect or disturb me.

"What power could it have not given to it by a man?" I ask her.

"Women's medicine," Narinda says.

In this nearly empty house I feel more support than I did surrounded by the Family.

"Give up everything," Lord Sean had said, "and come with us."

I had to do that to find out what remained that I couldn't give away.

Byron calls at 8 the next morning. I hear his voice, "Lily . . ." husky and round like his body. My heart pounds. He says it's my decision to make, but he wants to see me.

"You do? Why?" My voice sounds weak. The house feels cold. I wish I had a sweater.

"I want to talk to you. I'll be there in an hour."

"OK." I hang up the phone.

I ask Narinda what I should do. When she's serious, her jowls grow heavy and everything droops—earrings, ponytail, lower lip.

"Do you want to see him?" she asks, looking into my eyes like a motherly bloodhound.

"I guess I have to. I should." My stomach hurts. I'm shivering. The house is so cold; those foot-thick walls hold in the night air. I'm rubbing my chapped lower lip against the back of my thumb, my head turning slowly from side to side.

"There's no should about it. It just depends on what you feel."

"I don't know what I feel," I say, vaguely aware of tightness in my chest as if I were holding my breath.

The white Chevy van pulls up outside. I watch through the front window as Byron gets out and crosses in front of it to the walkway. He has driven to town by himself—no young lieutenant chauffeur today. The aspens out front tremble silver in the morning breeze. He knocks on the door and Narinda lets him in.

He stands near the door, dark against the white adobe wall. He's wearing his brown leather jacket and no beanie. His wispy hair, thinning on top, gives him a hint of vulnerability. But Narinda blocks him, as if guarding me.

"I can't see your light," Narinda tells him. I don't know what she means. Their eyes lock. She looks down first and moves away, crossing into the adjacent room and leaving the door ajar. The house is totally still.

"Lily," he says, taking a step toward me, "Everybody's surprised you're leaving."

"Surprised?" I back up. "Leanne and Noah knew. April knew. I told Daniel too." I wonder if he is angry.

He advances on me. "They love you. They said you're getting in the groove, you're really with us."

"But I'm not really." My voice quavers.

Inside, I'm hearing their voices intoning, "No one ever really leaves the Family."

Byron plants himself in front of me, stocky and broadchested, his face unreadable, at least to me. He takes a breath:

"I want you to come back with me."

But I can't breathe. Why me? When Don and Stephanie left, no one went after them. In fact, they congratulated Don for making the first clear decision of his life.

"When we were together in Iowa City," Byron says, "I felt closer to you than I ever had to any other woman." For a moment I remember the feel of his body, the lovemaking; for a moment I feel a rush of joy. He's saying he loves me and he recognizes me as his equal, his consort. For a second my ego puffs up and preens. But wait—closer to me than April, Maya, Isabel—the women who have been with him since the Family started? I know this is bullshit. He sees my disbelief and the veil comes down.

"That will never be again," Byron says.

He begins to destroy me in the only way it's done in the Family— by telling me who I am. He hurls his thunderbolts, a light-brown Zeus with hard hazel eyes.

"When you told me you loved me, you really hated me. You have never loved anyone."

"That's not true." Bullshit, I think, bullshit. But I'm wavering. I have no idea what love is.

"You will end by killing yourself."

I sink down into my personal abyss of thoughts chasing thoughts. I can't answer. I'm so fucked up!

"You have no idea who you're dealing with," he says. He's intent on telling me everything I've failed to understand, the things I've found so alien that I let them slide out of my memory. What is the Family really about? Why is Byron the man on top?

"I am the messiah," he says in a perfectly normal, firm voice. "When the apocalypse comes, I will lead the people out of the rubble."

Nothing I heard before, not even the insanity of the titles ceremony, prepared me for this. Not even the organism of many who act as one, not the astral projection, none of that. I am willing to listen, willing to believe in the possibility of experience that exceeds the limits of what we think we know. I believe that Arthur means something real when he says he can hear others' thoughts. I just don't know what it is, and I'm willing to live with that, to bracket it as something I don't understand but that is potentially understandable. I believe that I myself have had strange moments, that I have perceived what I have no name for, like the inter-dimensionality I saw across the desert on the way to Tucson, like the way the air had texture when I took LSD or mescaline. But an ordinary man saying he is a messiah, that goes beyond the pale. Even for me.

"The messiah? I can't believe you said that."

"I am a physician, a healer."

"You're a witch doctor," I say. He starts as if I have slapped him. I have used a term that is not consciously negative in anthropology. Witch doctor, shaman, healer—these are positive roles in traditional societies. But, on the other hand, this is not a traditional society.

"You can't see me as I am," he says, "as a human being. You only see the color of my skin. You think like a racist. And so does your friend." He means Narinda.

"Well, I'm not going back with you," I say, looking him straight in the eye, flushing, my heart racing. He looks surprised and scowls. I hold the stare. I'd rather die than give in. Even if I'm wrong.

A stubborn rage fills my chest and throat. I'm not crying, for once. My whole body is alive with a sense of myself and this place, of my feet on the wooden floor, my breath pulling in strength from the air.

"All right, then," he says. "So be it." Without dropping his eyes, he turns toward the door, as a cat leaves a fight without conceding.

The van starts up and Byron drives away. Narinda comes out of the adjacent room. I'm shaking, but I'm still hot with the finality of what I've done.

"He had such a bad vibration I was afraid to leave him alone with you. That's why I kept this door open."

Since Narinda is psychic, she must know something I don't; but I never thought he would hurt me physically. Just the other way. The Family's special form of total acceptance. Something like this: "We love you and accept you completely even though you are a worthless piece of shit."

And I think Byron is right about me. It's my guilt, my torment, that I'm white, middle class, and Protestant, with racists on both sides. I don't even know how to talk about my fears. I'm as culture bound as any redneck, which Narinda, with her Texas drawl and her square dance outfits, certainly is. I'm a pitiful cripple, a white woman in western civilization. But I'm free.

The footprints run crisscross

16

Nine at the beginning means:
The footprints run crisscross.
If one is seriously intent, no blame.

It is early morning and work begins. The mind has been closed to
the outside world in sleep; now its connections with the world begin
again. The trace of one's impressions run crisscross.

—*I Ching*, Chapter 30. *Li*/The Clinging, Fire

The heat of taking a stand against Byron gradually cooled into fear. I sat
down on Narinda's couch and sorted through my options, mostly internal. I was afraid I was crazy to have seen in this man something so different from what everyone else—and particularly the women—saw. I
was afraid of being wrong, afraid of being bad, afraid of losing love and
living forever alone. The next step seemed clear; I needed to find out the
answer to one basic question.

"Narinda," I said, "Do you know a psychiatrist?"

"What for?"

"I want to see one. Maybe I'm crazy."

"I don't think you're crazy, but if you want to see a psychiatrist I'll help you with that," she said.

In an hour or so she came to my room and said she had the name of a psychiatrist in Farmington, New Mexico, a town up in the northwest corner of the state, and she would be glad to drive me there if I made an appointment. She had somebody she wanted to visit in Farmington.

The earliest appointment I could get was four days away. Narinda got on the phone to her friend, made her arrangements and decided to leave the next day. We drove across northern New Mexico on narrow state highways, crossing the Jicarilla Apache Reservation in a late afternoon thunderstorm of purple sky and flashes of lightning. Approaching Farmington, Narinda told me that I would be staying in the town of Aztec, a few miles from Farmington. She would visit her friend and return to Taos, while I would stay with a Methodist minister and his wife to wait for my appointment.

"They're old friends of mine," she said. "He used to be the minister in Taos."

Homer and Betty Lou Reid lived in a squat pink house provided by the church on the edge of town (population about 1,000). A light wind blowing off the mesa tweaked the feathery mimosas that grew just beyond Homer and Betty Lou's lawn like challenges from the wild.

Homer was a ruddy-cheeked, bulky man with a beautiful tenor voice, as I discovered early the first morning in his house. He sang in the shower, not a few choruses of "Oh Susanna," but an aria from *the Magic Flute*. He sang so beautifully that my eyes filled with tears as I stood listening in the stark white hallway of the parsonage.

I followed the smell of bacon and biscuits into the kitchen. As Betty Lou set out the biscuits to cool, I asked if that was really Homer.

"Yes," she said, taking her time to set down the pan, wipe her hands, and fold the dish towel just so. She was slender and petite, a competent, kindly woman whose grown children's pictures adorned the hall. She wore lipstick but no other makeup, no fingernail polish, no fancy clothes. In contrast, the kitchen curtains sported cheerful red roosters, and a plastic bouquet of crimson flowers with flat green leaves perked up the kitchen table.

"Opera was his first love. He studied in Europe and sang all over the world before we met. He speaks five languages."

"Wow. But he quit that to become a minister?"

"No, it didn't quite happen that way. It was so hard to make a living at it, and when he married and had kids—we both were married before—he had to give it up. He made a living any old way for a while and it was quite a struggle." Betty Lou spoke softly, but her steady eyes gave me the impression she had a lot of backbone. "We each had three kids, and then we had our own son and daughter, so we had a large family to support."

Homer came into the kitchen, freshly shaved and jovial. He had pale blue eyes with light lashes and brows and a receding hairline. His head shone in the morning light. He put his arm around his wife, and the two of them stood before me as if for a family portrait.

"Had to keep the kids in bacon and biscuits," he said. "And besides, I love the church. I love the preaching." He chuckled. "Sometimes I do sermons in song, too. It's a good life."

Betty Lou patted him and turned toward the stove. She asked me if I'd like cereal or would I be willing to share their country breakfast?

"Are you kidding? I'd love it." It seemed impossible to express enough gratitude for this bounty. After breakfast, Homer went to his office at the church and I helped with the dishes and sat and talked a while with Betty Lou.

The church had moved them around a lot, she said; they had lived in small towns in Florida, Kansas, Oregon, and now, New Mexico.

"The bishop sends us to help out churches that have been having problems. Homer can go in and charm everybody and get them all pulling together. He's really good at that. Here in Aztec before we came, the average attendance was around twenty-five. He filled the church in two months. But he's a little too unusual for some of these congregations," she confided. "It starts well, but after a year or two somebody gets uncomfortable and then pretty soon he gets a message from the bishop that they're sending us on. I wish they would put him in a larger place where people would understand him better and appreciate him."

"You mean he's too liberal?"

"Well, not exactly that, although it's true he's a city boy and they always put us in the country. But you see, Homer and I were both baptized in the Holy Spirit, and in some churches we had healing meetings."

"I didn't think Methodists went in for that sort of thing." Pretty much all I knew of the Christian charismatics came from a documentary film, *Holy Ghost People,* used in anthropology courses. I loved that film, however, and carried indelible images of the people in it who went into trances, spoke in tongues, and handled rattlesnakes.

Betty Lou bridled. "It's very much a part of Methodism. John Wesley in England received the baptism of the Holy Spirit. It means you have a lot more understanding of what you believe in because you experience it directly.

"All my life I lived with the idea that there's someone up there taking care of me, and I have to be good. And I was. When I was a teenager I went hiking by myself in the mountains outside of Colorado Springs, and . . . I sat on a rock for a while, and I felt this enfolding warmth, and I knew it was the Holy Spirit."

Since I myself had had what I thought of as a mystical experience sitting on a rock in the mountains of Colorado, I felt I understood what she was talking about, despite the fact that I would not call it God. Although Betty Lou and Homer represented everything I thought of as "straight," I could see that they lived from the heart. They radiated the kindness and warmth of which she spoke.

"What about Aztec?" I asked. "It looks like a conservative town."

"It is. But we've gotten pretty good acceptance in Aztec, so I guess we'll be here a while."

She had things to do, and I decided to walk out to the Anasazi ruins, incorrectly called Aztec, that gave the town its name. It was already hot. There was no shade along the road. A high mesa broke up the far horizon; nearby the landscape was a jumble of eroded gullies and reddish boulders strewn around by millennia of wind. The ruins stretched out along a low hill that kept them out of the floodplain but in sight of the Animas River. The Old Ones understood the needs of the river; otherwise it would have swept away their traces. There was a small, deserted parking lot surrounded by a low adobe wall, and a closed-up visitor center. An interpretive sign said there were probably more people living there a thousand years ago than today. I seemed to be the only living human present.

I sat on a red adobe wall in the shade of a pepper tree listening to the voices in my head, more recent than the Anasazi. "No one ever really leaves the Family." "You'd better find somebody you can trust or else burn out your mind." "When we first met you, I knew you were in the Void." But there were other voices, too; Daniel saying he'd always be there for me; Arthur saying, "Trust yourself." And memories without words, of Leanne's clear, solemn gaze, Noah's smile, April's calm way of moving through the house.

A magpie coasted in and lit on a branch above me, making it sway as if tossed by a breeze. Asphalt black and arctic white in the sun, it chuckled and chattered, then opened its beak and commanded me to get off its wall. One black feather stuck out at a wrong angle from one wing, and yet this bird bounced on its branch, perfectly balanced and ready to arm-wrestle me off its territory. No shame for its imperfection.

After a while I gave in and moved along, working my way through the quiet alleys between half-rooms, half-walls, and the still-sacred spaces of these relatives of Chaco. When I found my way back to the entrance, a Park Service truck was parked at the back of the visitor center and the door was open. The main attraction inside was a rack of Navajo rugs, well-chosen and of high quality. I passed my hand over a thunder and lightning pattern, a Two Grey Hills. . . . Wondering who made these and who sold them . . . . Later in the afternoon, back at Homer and Betty Lou's, I took a nap.

There was a potluck supper at the church that night, and Homer and Betty Lou invited me to go with them. She said she thought her daughter's clothes would fit me, if I wanted to wear something else, but I decided to go in my own peasant blouse and skirt.

"Will it bother you to bring a hippie to the potluck?" I asked. Betty Lou's eyes lit up with a big smile.

"Not a bit," she said. "I'm proud of you for choosing to be yourself."

The church was a 1950s whitewashed stucco building on a quiet street (the only kind of street there was in Aztec). We walked downstairs and into a long basement room with fans going at either end, and tables set up with white butcher paper. The fans blew a warm food scent around. I thought I smelled hamburger, perhaps mixed with mushroom soup. Church ladies milled around between kitchen and main room, and about twenty or thirty people ranging from old folks to toddlers sat, stood, fanned themselves, waited for food. A young mother shepherded a tow-headed boy and girl of about eight, who looked like twins, to set their offerings of breadsticks and Velveeta onto the food table. There were dishes of potato salad, green and red jello, cold cuts, white bread, carrot and celery sticks, and a few casseroles, one with a baked-on cornflake topping.

A couple of large middle-aged women greeted Homer as if they genuinely liked him, and welcomed Betty Lou, and then me, with unreserved warmth. An elderly couple beamed at us as if they had already arrived at the gates of Heaven. It was hard to imagine any tension over Homer's ministry here; his flock loved him. After a hearty meal we helped with the cleanup, folded the tables, and stacked the chairs. Back at home, Betty Lou turned on the TV. It was about time for *Gunsmoke*.

The next day I wandered around town some more and went back to the Reids' hoping to find something to read. They had a local newspaper, a wide selection of Christian books, and some of the classics—Dickens, Shakespeare, Wharton. I picked up *Of Human Bondage*, which I hadn't read since high school, and settled in. After dinner we watched TV again. A family was in crisis; there was a loud argument, shots, someone fell to the floor. The daughter saw her father's body and screamed hysterically. The police came. One comforted the girl. I looked around at the Reids' living room, so tidy, clean, and peaceful. All the drama was on the screen. In the life I had recently left, the drama was happening every day, in the people. I missed them. I missed waking up in the lower bunk, hearing stirrings all around me; company in the kitchen, sharing cooking, sharing meals, even company doing the dishes. I missed the hugs and the eye contact and the loud laughs, the shrieks, maybe not the accusations, but I missed the excitement of it and the constant stirrings of the heart.

Finally it was time for my appointment and Homer took me into Farmington to see the psychiatrist. Dr. Hutchins was dressed in business-casual for a small western town: a blue cotton shirt, Levis, and cowboy boots. His office was equally unpretentious, with a couple of framed degrees on the wall, a bookshelf, a telephone, and Venetian blinds trimmed down against the morning sun.

"I thought I should see a psychiatrist," I began, "because I've been living in a commune and everyone else loves the leader of it, but I hate him."

He raised one eyebrow.

"So? Tell me a little about your background. How did you get here? Where are you from? Where is your family?"

I gave him a short version of how I joined the commune and how I ended up in his office. I told him I was headed back to Boulder to pick up my things, and possibly to Boston after that. He wanted to know more about the commune.

"Do they use drugs?"

"No, we have a rule against drugs. No drugs. Not even alcohol."

Another eyebrow flash. "That's unusual. So drugs aren't involved. Go on."

"You have to change your name and give up all your possessions."

"What did you have?"

"Oh, I don't know, not much. I left my books and records in Boulder. I just had a sleeping bag and a camera and some clothes. And about a hundred dollars."

"And you gave them all that?"

"Well, yeah, but I got other clothes, and I kept the camera. My father sent me a check and that's how I was able to leave."

"Where is your father?"

"My father lives in Yucaipa, California. My mother is in Los Angeles. They divorced when I was ten. He remarried, so I have a stepmother. My mother never remarried. I think maybe she hates men." He didn't pick up on that one.

"Do you have any brothers and sisters?"

"No. I'm an only child."

"Hm. And who is this man you hate?"

"He's the leader of the commune. Lord Byron. That's his current name. He's black, and he's an ex-con. He's a very charming man but when I spent some time alone with him we argued all the time."

"Tell me again why you thought you needed to see a psychiatrist?"

"I thought I might be crazy, because I hated Byron and everybody else loves him. The women love him. 'Byron's far out.' 'You'll love him,' they said."

"And why do you hate him?"

"I think he makes bad decisions for the group. He went to New York and was staying in hotels and using our credit cards when we didn't have any money for food at home in Taos. We were eating pancakes every day because we couldn't afford to buy meat or vegetables. It was even hard to get milk and meat for the children. We're $20,000 in debt and Byron thinks it's okay not to pay it back and make other people deal with it. The little, gentle people have to suffer because of him."

The psychiatrist shifted in his chair and looked away from me, toward the sunlight spilling around the edges of the drawn blinds. I felt, in the silence, my own hot face and sweaty palms.

"Also, he has the right to sleep with all of the women," I said.

"Including you?"

"Yes."

"Did he use force?"

"No." Dr. Hutchins scrutinized me. I sat still and didn't add any more details. He hmmed again.

"It sounds like you have plenty to be angry about. Is there something wrong with being angry?"

I sucked in my breath. Apparently I had been holding it for a while.

"Well, yes. Theoretically I suppose it's all right to be angry but I don't know when. I mean in general, no, I feel bad when I'm angry."

"You feel bad?"

"Yes. I feel like I'm bad to be angry. I shouldn't get mad at other people."

"You shouldn't? According to whom?"

"According to my mother, for one thing. And me. I don't like it when I get mad, it doesn't feel right to me. I don't know what to do. How do you know if you're right, when you're angry?"

He paused again, looking at me as if solving a geometry problem.

"Dealing with anger isn't easy."

I breathed again.

"These are valid questions you're asking. But you're not crazy."

"I'm not?"

"No. Of course not."

I waited for more. He looked back calmly.

"Anger inevitably arises in all relationships. We all have to deal with it, but it's not something I can solve for you in an hour. When you get to wherever you're going, if you still want help with this, you can look for some counseling. You don't need a psychiatrist."

"Oh."

"You've stayed in touch with your parents?"

"Yes."

"You have friends here and friends to go to in Boulder?"

"Yes."

"You're doing all right, as far as I can see. Good luck."

He smiled and stood up. I walked out of the office and into the bright heat. Homer's old Chevy was at the curb.

Betty Lou said I could get a ride to Boulder in the morning with the boys who drove the milk truck.

"They're nice boys," she said. "We know their families."

It felt right to me. In the Family, I had gotten used to following the flow, and this definitely felt like the flow. The truck pulled up to the back door at six in the morning. I hugged Homer, hugged Betty Lou, and climbed in.

The road north out of Aztec, New Mexico follows the Animas River. The guy driving the milk truck called it "the river of lost souls."

"Why?" I asked. "*Animas* just means souls in Spanish. Why should they be lost?"

"I dunno." He kept his eyes on the road. Red-orange and burnt sienna earth rolled by; the engine labored. "Out here it just seems like any souls that would be out here would be lost."

At around noon we drove into the town of Ouray, deep in a steep-sided, red cliff canyon, a river along the valley floor, and waterfalls coming off the sides of the canyon. Its beauty overwhelmed me. The sunlight playing on the red and gold cliffs danced in mysteries. "This is it," I told the boys. "I have to get out here."

The clinging, fire

17

A luminous thing giving out light must have within itself something that perseveres; otherwise it will in time burn itself out. Everything that gives light is dependent on something to which it clings . . . Thus sun and moon cling to heaven, and grain, grass and trees cling to the earth.

—*I Ching*, Chapter 30. *Li*/The Clinging, Fire

Ouray, Colorado nestled along a narrow river valley with red rock cliffs all around. Towering over it to the west, a ribbon of white water cascaded down a granitic precipice. The main street was a mix of old buildings in need of repair and others that had been rehabilitated to look like the even Older West. I booked a room for $15 in the Ouray Hotel and followed the clerk up creaking wooden stairs to a sparsely furnished room with a window looking down on the street. Late afternoon light gilded the town.

The clerk recommended a small restaurant a block up the street, which, like the hotel, was built of unpainted, weathered wood. It felt unpretentious and homey. Potted plants and flowers were the only decorations. There were a few other young diners in blue jeans and cotton, and an older couple who shared a newspaper. I had a fresh salad garnished with sunflower seeds and a green chile enchilada, the first time I'd had such tasty, healthful food since leaving Seattle to join Byron in Iowa City.

The waiter, a man in his thirties with sandy hair and permanently arched eyebrows, was also the cook and the owner. I asked if he needed a waitress. He said he had a couple of shifts available. Kaleidoscopic images flared up: myself waiting on tables, cheerful, calm; hiking up a trail in sunshine, a nice man at my side; settling into a quiet life in a beautiful small town. I filled out an application, and he said he could let me know the next day. He seemed straightforward, easy to talk to.

"What's this town like?" I asked him.

"It's a mining town," he said. "Silver mining. And we also mine the tourists."

"Do you get much tourism? It looks pretty quiet."

"We get by." He looked at my application—no address or phone number—and looked more closely at me. "Are you sure you're going to stick around?"

My chest felt suddenly hollow. I couldn't answer.

"If I do, I'll need a job." He accepted that without comment. He said I could find out more about the town in the morning at the Chamber of Commerce information booth.

"It's in a little red caboose about a block up that way. You can't miss it."

I bought a newspaper and returned to my room for the night. The occasional cars on the street below passed at a pedestrian pace.

Out of the night's deep sleep this dream emerged:

I'm driving on a highway in the Southwest with a kind companion beside me. We are passing through a desert valley that I recognize from other dreams. The light has the extraordinary clarity that comes after a rain. On the left I can see high mountains of red earth and the mottled green of trees, and all around us a cerulean sky. Beside the road stands a rosy, sunset-colored bird with a slender, black beak. We know it is there for us; it is a sign.

The little red caboose, holding nothing more than a display of tourist brochures and a counter, opened early. Inside stood a woman of about sixty, dressed all in white. Her neck was wrinkled, as if she had lived in the sun a long time, but her gray and black hair fluffed out around her face like a girl's.

"Hello, dear," she said, and scrutinized me with green eyes. "Oh my, you *are* in the Void, aren't you?"

There it was again. I had a vague understanding of "the Void" as a Buddhist term. I had read Alan Watts and D. T. Suzuki on Zen Buddhism in high school and had been introduced to the practice of zazen—sitting meditation—when I was a freshman at the University of Hawaii. Robert and Anne Aitken's home in Honolulu, called Koko An, formed the center of a small zen community. For the Aitkens, Buddhism was a path for becoming more, not less, involved in the world. The touchstone for them was compassion, the way of the bodhisattvas who attain enlightenment but then choose to stay on the wheel of birth, death, and rebirth in order to help others and reduce suffering. Anne's kind letters pursued me for years after I left Hawaii, urging me to find my own way through service to others. I thought I should want to do that, but I didn't.

"What are you seeking?" the Chamber of Commerce woman asked me.

"I don't know," I said. "I guess I'm looking for home." She nodded. I told her I had left a commune in Taos and was thinking of visiting friends and relatives in Boston.

"Maybe this is your home," she said.

"Maybe it is." A silence fell and I wondered how I would know. As if reading my thoughts, she spoke again:

"You will know by the end of the day, if you truly ask for that knowing. And if you ask for a sign. Have you ever used a pendulum?"

"Used a pendulum? No. What for?"

She smiled with serene authority, bent down and brought out a small box from under the counter. She opened it and told me to choose the one I felt drawn to. Inside it were three small objects of different shapes and sizes on necklace-length cords. One was a silver pendant with zigzag edges like a flower, set with an amber stone. Yellow isn't my best color, so I knew I wouldn't want that one and looked at the next. It was some kind of carved stone in a simple teardrop shape that I thought was rather ugly. The third was an odd, elongated shape with a bulb at the bottom, carved of burnished wood with a colorful grain. It held a tiny vial, visible through oblong windows carved into the neck.

She spoke again. "The vial is to carry an essential oil. You should choose one that gives you clarity."

My hand reached out and took it from the box. I enclosed the smooth wood in my palm and wrapped the black cord around my other hand. This one felt right.

"What do you do with it?" I asked.

"You have to find out if it's willing to work with you. Hold it up with one hand. Either hand." Doubtfully, I held the cord in my right hand and dangled the pendulum in front of me.

"You need an agreement on what will be yes and what will be no. Ask it to show you a yes."

"Huh?"

"Say it out loud."

"Show me a yes," I said, directing my attention to the pendulum. Nothing happened. I looked at her uncertainly.

"Put some energy into wanting it. Do you want this to work? Do you want to have a way to contact your intuition?"

Of course I wanted to contact my intuition.

"You haven't done that too much, have you?"

I certainly hadn't, when it came to my own life, although I trusted my intuition when it came to intellectual tasks. When I was doing anthropological field work in Colombia, I used to think of the preliminary process as "filling up my intuition." Perhaps others would call it "doing your homework." I would observe people, ask questions, and find out all sorts of things without knowing what it all meant. I knew that eventually if I asked the right question of myself, the answer would pop into my head. To me, analysis was a mystery, more like channeling than an act of will. If I knew enough of the various pieces, the whole picture would emerge. I trusted that process. But when it came to personal choices, such as whether to stay or go, I felt totally adrift.

"When I have to make a decision like this, I don't know how to figure it out."

"There's your problem," she said. "You can't figure it out because it's not something you do with your head. You make your life decisions with your heart. Now try again."

I looked at the pendulum. Monkey mind (another Buddhist concept) chattered away: My heart, my heart, not my head, my head. For a second the chatter died down and my only thought was—

"Show me a yes."

The pendulum swung toward me and away, back and forth in an unmistakable arc. I laughed in amazement. The woman told me to thank it, and I did.

"Show me a no." It hung there until I thought it wouldn't work a second time; then it began swaying gently from side to side. I stared at my hand. I could detect no movement in the fingers and thumb holding the cord, nor in the hand itself. I looked at the woman again; her emerald eyes flashed. I realized I would have to buy this thing.

"I can let you have it for five dollars," she said.

My $100 was going fast, but I figured I'd either get a job and stay, or go to Boulder on the bus. Either way the money would work out. So I paid her.

She gave me some additional instructions: I was to take the pendulum home and get comfortable with it by asking easy questions, such as "Do I like chocolate?" I was to wear it constantly so it could "get used to my energy." And I should preface the serious questions with something like this: "Is it to my highest good . . ." or "I'm sincerely asking guidance on. . . ." The notion of guidance from a piece of wood didn't bother me. I knew I needed help.

The woman also gave me a tip about another place to work. She said there was a doctor in Ouray who gave high colonic treatments and owned a hot springs with healing waters. He had rental cabins for his patients there, and I might get a job cleaning cabins. She told me how to find the place and said that if he was there, and if he had a job for me, it would be a sign. Presumably, if he wasn't, or if he didn't, it would also be a sign. . . . She implied that I would know when the time came whether I was to stay or go.

I asked if she was a Buddhist. She said she had studied Theosophy for many years and was now a member of a metaphysical sect called "the I Am." I didn't really want to know more. It was enough that this town employed a metaphysician to run its Chamber of Commerce.

I wandered down a side street to find the "doctor's" establishment. The street was paved but had no sidewalks, and the modest, weathered houses looked like summer homes. Scattered hollyhocks and bachelor's buttons gave a touch of color, but I saw no serious gardens and nobody working outside in the cool morning air. A blue car parked in the driveway of a grey-shingled bungalow suggested someone lived there, and I thought I saw a movement through the window, but other than that I felt alone on this street. At the next corner I saw a row of dingy, pale yellow cottages. The one at the end was larger, like a mother goose leading a row of goslings, and a sign on the door said "Dr. John Payson, please ring bell." I rang, but no one answered. I knocked but there was no response. I stood on the porch for a while in the vague sunlight, wondering what to do. Ah—the pendulum. I took it off my neck and held it up. "I'd really like guidance on this," I murmured to it. "Shall I wait for the doctor to come back and try to get a job here?" My little talisman swung from side to side. No. I noticed a feeling of agreement somewhere inside me. I didn't want to stay here—in the terms of the woman in the red caboose, I didn't feel drawn to this place. I walked away, satisfied.

A trail to the waterfall on the cliff above the town started a block or two above the main street, and I headed for it. The trail climbed quickly. It hugged the cliff, suspended in places on a heavy scaffolding of wooden beams and packed rock. It looked as though it had been built by the miners. Several times I stopped to catch my breath and turned to look out over the valley. These looked like the mountains in my dream, the intense reds of the earth and the greens of the timber sharply defined against the sky. I hastened up the trail, almost ran up it in spite of the altitude. The waterfall must have been above 8,000 feet, since the town itself was at 7,700. White water shot out of a gap in the rock at least 100 feet above my head, like a hole in the sky, and fanned down over a vertical garden. Where the water lost force and turned into spray, it created niches for green hanging plants. Where it fell thick and heavy as liquid rock, my eyes followed it down until it crashed into foam, then followed it up to start falling over and over. It's hard to think when you stand so close to a water creature so immense, and I didn't try to think. In fact, I let go. I sat down by the pool in a bright fog of spray tossed in sunlight and just counted senses; feet in shoes with toes sticking up, legs and bottom on rocky pebbles, my warm inner body miraculously held up by muscle and skeleton, arms free and hands in lap, head balanced nicely on clever, flexible neck, hair pulled back and twisted and getting wet. Cool spray on skin; moist, sweet air coming in and going out; eyes seeing ravens high against the sky, calling, but their voices captured in the water's roar. After a good long while I stood up and walked back down the trail.

In late afternoon, I returned to the restaurant. The owner said I could have the job, lunch and dinner four days a week. I felt clear that I didn't want it. I thanked him and said I had decided not to stay. The bus for Boulder arrived from the south at about 6:30, and I stepped on.

Afterword

The Family left Taos sometime in late summer of 1970, literally in the middle of the night. I first heard about this from Narinda, the Taos artist, with whom I remained in contact. In recent years, while sorting through my own memories for this book, I made several trips to New Mexico in hope of finding out more. I didn't really want to find former members of our group; the saying, "No one ever really leaves the Family" remained faintly ominous to my ears and I didn't want to test it. It turned out to be difficult to find anybody in Taos thirty years later who remembered much about them.

Finally, I was fortunate to be able to contact Charles Lonsdale. It was Charles's own money that started the Lorien Foundation, the source of funding for the Family's film, and also for the General Store, the Information Center, much of the Free Clinic, and even the Gallery House. Charles also helped start *The Fountain of Light*, the Taos counter-culture's newspaper, and in general contributed enormous creative energy, good sense, and goodwill to the community that encompassed the hippies and the town. In April 2002, Charles was staying in Los Angeles, and I was on my way home after a visit to Taos. We met and talked for a while on a sunny afternoon. His daughter, Athena, born in 1970, and her two large, furry dogs sat with us on the lawn or wandered off for a while and came back to listen.

"They [the Family] didn't say goodbye to anybody," Charles recalled. "They cleaned the Gallery House meticulously. It was immaculate—

ready for the next owner. They piled up three dumptruck loads of stuff—old clothes, broken toys, cribs, etc.—in the yard. They did it in the middle of the night and left before dawn. It was a surprise. Like you know a tree is rotting and you know it's going to fall sometime soon, but still the day it falls it's a surprise."

I asked what he remembered of the Family and what he thought of them.

"I remember they were hardworking and well-organized. Byron had a clear idea of what needed to be done and he kept them focused. That was quite an accomplishment in those days. A lot of people were into just hanging out."

Lonsdale moved to Taos in 1968 from Haight Ashbury. "The local people were saying, 'Oh, these hippies will go back to San Francisco once the winter sets in.' But every other day there was another busload of kids—all looking for a place to stay. I saw what needed to be done."

Among many other projects, he helped find or build housing for the incoming hordes.

"At that time, Taos had a lot of vacant houses—at least 200 vacant houses. It was a matter of knocking on doors, finding out who the owner was—it was usually somebody's sister or father or something like that—and for $50 or $100 you could rent a house in varying states of serious disrepair. And each little (hippie) family would fix them up, and then when they had shelter they'd look for the next thing, food, and then work. They would wind up at the General Store, where there was something to do and a way to earn a little money. Byron pretty much was the kingpin to manage all that. I started it, but it wouldn't have happened without his leadership."

In the Family, Lorien was mentioned occasionally as the rather mysterious source of money for the film. It was called a foundation or a project or just Lorien, and I inferred it was something like a Digger project, philanthropy to build a new community without the old rules. But Lorien was much more than that. As Charles described in an interview in *Scrapbook of a Taos Hippie*, by Iris Keltz, published in 2000, it was also a piece of land, a commune on fifty acres north of Taos, a construction company, and, today, a farming cooperative. The Lorien project, in those heady days, Charles told me, "was like riding a wild horse without a halter or saddle—we were just on the back of this wild horse trying to hang on." The ride lasted about two years, from 1968 to 1970.

"There was a point when the local folks turned from hospitable to hostile," Lonsdale said (just about the point when I joined the commune). "They felt overwhelmed. At the end of 1968 there were two communes. At the end of 1969 there were fifty-five communes. At the end of 1970 there were three communes—Lama, New Buffalo, and the Magic Tortoise."

By the end of 1970 the General Store was gone, too. "Once we ran out of money everything folded at the same time," Lonsdale said.

I told him about Narinda's party. "Yeah, the artists saved us," he said. "Otherwise we would've been massacred. They understood creative chaos."

He asked me if I had seen Byron since leaving the Family in 1970.

"No," I said, "I didn't want to." Charles said he wasn't surprised. His own parting with Byron was hostile.

"We were out of money and he wanted to go to the bank and make a ruse and get whatever we needed. I didn't agree; I wasn't willing to go along with that."

I thought of what little I knew of the Family's finances. The Lord Family credit card, the credo that "money is just energy." I had been told that Lorien had given us a grant of $20,000 to make the film, but Lonsdale said it was $70,000, an enormous sum at the time.

"What do you think of Byron now?" I asked him. "Was he a good person, a bad person, a mixed person?"

"He was a very complex person," Lonsdale said. "He had leadership skills, he was charismatic, and also he was . . ." He paused and looked off toward the palm trees at the edge of the lawn. Athena patted one of the dogs. "Not megalomaniac, but that authoritative personality," he said. "No, he wasn't a megalomaniac.

"But he would tell a different story every week. He was a paramedic, trained in some branch of the service. He was in the Parachute Corps. One time he told me (in a roomful of people) he was a full-blooded Indian." (In gestures he implied that people smiled, did doubletakes.) "Sure, Byron, you can be whatever you want to be."

And that was partly true. It's partly true for all of us, and I thank Byron and other members of the Family for planting the seed of that idea in me. I thank them also for helping me discover what I wanted and didn't want to be. I didn't want the same things they did, and that, as the *I Ching* says, is "no blame."

Small groups can be powerful vehicles of change, especially because of the power of attributions—the statements others make that define us, such as "You're nice," "you're crazy," "you're just like your father," and so on. Attributions are hypnotic suggestions, much more effective than commands.[3] They're everyday brainwashing. When we say someone is manipulative, as Byron was, we usually mean they're great at using attributions to put the other person on the defensive and get what they want.

While working on my master's thesis, I compared initiation into the Family with the process of Chinese Communist "brainwashing," or thought reform, also accomplished in small groups. The main difference was the degree of control and coercion. One could not simply get up and walk out of a Communist re-education group. The main similarity, however, was the big cognitive changes that could take place in a short time. These changes could be temporary if they didn't fit with a convert's previous identity, and if they weren't supported by the social environment afterwards; but they could be far-reaching if the group closed itself off from any outside influence. Despite the Family's role of service in the community, for most of its members the Family was a small and inward-focused world that exerted strong pressure for conformity and change.

The Family had more porous boundaries than many such groups, for which I am grateful, and I believe it was founded and organized with good intentions. The fact that I experienced the group as coercive had as much to do with me as with others. That is always the case. A person always has choices about how to deal with coercive situations. Sometimes the options are much uglier than mine were. As Byron himself told me, all I had to do to get my freedom was take it. Sometimes it's harder than that. Nevertheless, there's always a choice.

It was my great good fortune to have a father who persisted in writing me his newsy letters with checks enclosed, even when he knew I was

---

3.   Described as such by R.D. Laing in *The Politics of the Family*, Pantheon Books, 1969.

likely to give the money away. He had faith in me when I had absolutely no faith in him. I can only infer that my companions who repeatedly called themselves misfits and losers really did feel that they had nowhere else to go and no other support. That would have made them much more vulnerable to the group's influence. And besides, there was so much to gain by staying—love and companionship and sex and the security that comes from not having to make all of one's own decisions. As many social critics have pointed out, our American extreme emphasis on individuality deprives us of some of the basic satisfactions of being human.

When I left the Family, I was in an altered state of consciousness, truly in the mind-state of a pilgrim. I made a pilgrimage to Boston to seek out "the best in our society," the values that were denied or denigrated in the Family. I believed that there were successful people of humanistic intelligence who could be admirable even though they were part of the mainstream. I stayed initially with an aunt and uncle who were kind and supportive, then contacted a professor and writer whose books I admired, and who I believed might embody those qualities I was seeking. He and his wife listened to my story, opened their hearts and their considerable network of friends to me, helped me find work and a safe place to live, and encouraged me to write about the Family. My mentors didn't press me to return to graduate school. It was I who decided to take that step, driven by the fear that I would be a failure if I didn't.

When I started writing about the commune, I found that both my handwriting and my writing style had changed; the sentences were shorter, the concepts simpler. I thought of it as a change in my mental furniture; I had tossed out the excessively complex jargon of academia and moved in the excessively simple jargon of the Family.

The Family opened some doors to the parts of the universe that didn't fit into my academic worldview, however, and over the years I have returned to those doors, and, occasionally, walked through. I still consult the *I Ching*, although I don't always follow its advice. Like the Bible, it contains wisdom for every conceivable human condition. I still have great respect for Fritz Perls and his colleagues and the theory and practice of Gestalt therapy.

Two years after I left the commune, I found a Gestalt therapist in Tacoma, Washington, Karl Humiston, M.D., trained by Perls, whose work helped me enormously. His practice, to be honest, bore very little resemblance to anything I went through in the Family. (I think Samantha's demonstration at the World Affairs Conference was as good as it ever got.) Humiston gave detailed instructions for how to get in touch with the body and notice one's sensory perceptions. This sounds so obvious, but is at the heart of the issue for so many of us trained since early childhood not to acknowledge any inconvenient truths. The style of working with dreams that Perls developed also was a key to my growth and learning. I loved Gestalt dreamwork, and still do, because of the principle that it is the dreamer who interprets the dream. I felt so little right to my own internal process that it was a profound moment when I realized that my dreams were my own and that Humiston wasn't going to tell me what they meant. He would just direct my attention to the various elements of the dream and allow me to dramatize them—to become them and speak from them and discover what was hidden in them, all for myself.

After about five years of college teaching and research, I resolved to leave academia. Several years of short-lived jobs followed: waitressing, proofreading, temp typing, copy editing, and then a long spate of technical writing. A few years after that I made another break, from the well-paid world of technical writing to "real" writing, i.e., working as a reporter on a small-town newspaper and then freelancing as a journalist. I've been writing one way or another ever since.

The World Affairs Conference is still held yearly on the University of Colorado campus in Boulder, and is still an unmatchable merry-go-round of big ideas. Its founder, Howard Higman, died in 1995, but the conference carries on under the leadership of second-generation conferees, people who love what it stands for. What it stands for was stated succinctly in a 1990 interview with Higman published in the *Los Angeles Times*.

> *"We do not intend to arrive at a solution or an answer or to come up with a proposal for anything," explained . . . Higman, a university sociologist. The conference's purpose is to provide a forum for ideas, to allow audiences to "observe intellectuals debating issues in public" and to "help people form their own opinions" about current events and contemporary issues, Higman said.*
>
> — *Los Angeles Times,* April 13, 1990

I attended the 2001 World Affairs Conference and found it every bit as fascinating as it was in 1970. This time, however, I didn't grab a brass ring, change my life or my name, or run off on a whole new adventure. I met interesting people, had intense conversations, took notes, and when it was over climbed back in my car and drove home. And that was enough.

Acknowledgments

The writing community of Fishtrap, in Enterprise, Oregon, and its executive director, Richard Wandschneider, provided the context, the encouragement, the catalyst, the opportunity, the friendship, the help, and even the time (through the Writers' Retreats) to write this book. I particularly thank the members of my writing groups in Portland and Enterprise, all related one way or another to Fishtrap, for their patient readings and responses to early drafts. I am grateful to Andrew Pham and Debra Earling, who, as teachers, made their own extraordinary gifts for living and writing seem accessible, maybe even contagious. My friend Amerinda Alpern put at my disposal her astonishing insights and unflagging enthusiasm for getting to the heart of the matter. I thank my editor, Elizabeth Hadas, for her benevolence. Thanks to Suzanne Smith, Beth Helstien, Peggy Risch, Benjamin Curry, Jeff Green, Tom Hampson, Monika Hunter, Gregg Kleiner, Lynn Sampson, Mary Slowik, Eileen Thiel, and Rich Wandschneider for their insightful comments, and to Sue Armitage for her advice. And thanks to Thelma Dodson, Betty Lou Reid, Nancy Harmon, Judith Rafferty, Siggie Bonnett, Danae Willson, and Leah, Zedeck, Arthur, and Daniel for being my friends through difficult times. Thanks to Harold and Viola Isaacs for enfolding me in their magic circle. Thank you.

Margaret Hollenbach is a free-lance writer in Ashland, Oregon.
© Nancy and Jerry Harmon, 2004.